"The book offers an amazing richness of knowledge as to how this Trinitarian mystery is alive and operative in the Church, especially in the Sacraments. I am particularly grateful for the further confirmation the author presents of the truth of Maria Montessori's statement early in the twentieth century that 'the liturgy is the magnificent teaching tool of the Church,' along with Sofia Cavalletti's and Gianna Gobbi's re-discovery of the centrality of the Bible-Liturgy unity in our life of faith, beginning with the youngest children and expanding throughout our life!"

—REBEKAH ROJCEWICZ, Executive Member of the International Council for the Catechesis of the Good Shepherd

"Earnest Skublics' *Plunged into the Trinity* could be read by anyone interested in religious ritual. But it should also be read by everyone who participates in and thinks about Christian sacramental life. With ecumenical breadth and catholic depth, this little book bears a scholar's learning and a pastoral heart. Its chapters on the Eucharist are feasts worthy of repeated enjoyment. Eat, drink, and be filled!"

—REVEREND FRANKLIN WILSON, retired pastor

"Ernest Skublics's book, *Plunged into the Trinity,* is an excellent resource for all involved in Christian religious education, and not just for the catechists following the catechetical methods of the Good Shepherd, with whom the chapters of this book originated as talks. Skublics is so well placed to provide such an outstanding instrument for catechesis. He has spent a lifetime studying and exploring liturgical and sacramental theology and, more importantly, actively participating in the liturgical assembly. His focus on Eucharistic ecclesiology, with the Eucharist as the beating heart of the church drawing us into the life of the Trinity, affords him a richly creative integrating focus for his reflections. Any catechist, indeed anyone interested in Christian theology, will benefit from this book, and not only from the well-informed historical and theological perspective provided by the author. They will benefit also from the lucidity with which the book is written (including its illustrative diagrams), as well as from its powerful ecumenical awareness. In respect of the latter Skublics draws insight and illustration from across the ecclesial spectrum—for example, from Metropolitan John Zizioulas,

Nikolai Afanassief (the Orthodox tradition), Paul McPartlan (Roman Catholic), Martin Luther and his great commentator Paul Althaus, and Geoffrey Wainwright (Methodist), among others. I cannot recommend it highly enough."

—Owen F. Cummings, Regents' Professor of Theology,
Mount Angel Seminary

Plunged into the Trinity

Plunged into the Trinity

Our Sacramental Becoming

ESSAYS IN
SACRAMENTAL ECCLESIOLOGY

ERNEST SKUBLICS
Foreword by ANN GARRIDO

 CASCADE *Books* • Eugene, Oregon

PLUNGED INTO THE TRINITY
Our Sacramental Becoming

Cascade Books
An Imprint of Wipf and Stock Publishers
199 W. 8th Ave., Suite 3
Eugene, OR 97401

www.wipfandstock.com

PAPERBACK ISBN: 978-1-5326-6609-4
HARDCOVER ISBN: 978-1-5326-6610-0
EBOOK ISBN: 978-1-5326-6611-7

Cataloguing-in-Publication data:

Names: Skublics, Ernest

Title: Plunged into the trinity : our sacramental becoming / Ernest Skublics.

Description: Eugene, OR: Cascade Books, 2019 | Series: if applicable | Includes bibliographical references and index.

Identifiers: ISBN 978-1-5326-6609-4 (paperback) | ISBN 978-1-5326-6610-0 (hardcover) | ISBN 978-1-5326-6611-7 (ebook)

Subjects: LCSH: Sacraments—Catholic Church. | Trinity. | Theological anthropology—Christianity.

Classification: BX2200 .S45 2019 (print) | BX2200 (ebook)

Manufactured in the U.S.A.   APRIL 12, 2019

I dedicate this little book to the Catechesis of the Good Shepherd Association of Canada, to whom some of this material was originally presented, as an expression of my admiration for their work, implementing their Montessori-inspired way of helping children fall in love with God and explore the lifelong adventure resulting from their intimate plunge into communion with him.

Table of Contents

Foreword xi

Chapter 1: Plunged into the Trinity 1

Chapter 2: Sacramental Realism and the Plunge 9

Chapter 3: The Covenantal Dynamic of the Eucharist 17

Chapter 4: The Eucharist Makes the Church 31

Chapter 5: Luther on the Eucharist and the Church 39

Chapter 6: Obedience and Love 45

Chapter 7: The Great Commandment of Communion 51

Chapter 8: Communion, Reconciliation, Public
and Private Sins 61

Chapter 9: Confession—the Sacrament of Spiritual Friendship 65

Chapter 10: The Church and Beyond in the Perspective
of Trinitarian Communion 67

Bibliography 79

Foreword

WHEN MY FAMILY GATHERS to celebrate a birthday, before the candles can be extinguished and the cake sliced, one among us reads what has become our traditional birthday blessing. In the middle, the reader pauses for the whole family to chime in together with a quote from the artist Pablo Picasso: "*It takes a long, long time for one to become young!*"

The older I grow the more clearly I understand the sentiment behind this statement. It takes a long time to become more fully who we have always been. It takes a long time to recover the joy and simplicity that marks childhood. It takes a long time to be as daring and free as we were in youth.

The Italian theologian Sofia Cavalletti describes a similar realization when she writes about the slow evolution of the Catechesis of the Good Shepherd movement. Discussing the twenty years of experimentation that finally led to a single but seminal presentation on the eucharistic presence of the Good Shepherd, she writes, "I think it took us so long to achieve this idea because it was so natural and essential. . . . Great things are simple; nevertheless, simplicity—true and essential—opens up horizons so limitless and profound that we feel almost lost when confronted with them."

It takes a long, long time for something to become simple.

This small book you now have before you shows all of the signs of a lengthy, refining journey. Ernest Skublics began his studies in liturgical theology at the famed Sant' Anselmo in Rome in the early 1960s, later continuing his studies at the University of Ottawa in Canada and the University of Nijmegen in the Netherlands. He studied under many of the most important theological figures of the twentieth century, including Cipriano Vagaggini, Balthasar Fischer, Edward Schillebeeckx, and Augustine Mayer. During his long academic career, he was active in Orthodox-Catholic and Catholic-Anglican dialogues, writing for distinguished theological journals in the US, Canada, and the UK. In 1993, he became the first lay dean of Mount Angel—a Benedictine seminary outside Salem, Oregon—helping to restructure the seminary's curriculum around the unifying framework of communion ecclesiology. Such vast learning and extensive experience could take a scholar in the direction of increased specialization and complexity, resulting in only a few other peers being able to read one's work. But Dr. Skublics—now in his eighties—has instead walked the path of Picasso and Cavalletti.

It takes a long, long time to produce a work of sacramental theology so essential and accessible.

In the pages that follow, Skublics synthesizes the substantive scholarship that undergirded the twentieth-century liturgical movement, bearing particular fruit in the Second Vatican Council. But, he does so in such a way that the "average person in the pew" will be able to readily grasp. Christian readers of every stripe will be moved by the way Skublics illumines the simultaneous simplicity and profundity of the sacraments. As such, this book makes a wonderful companion to the writings of Sofia Cavalletti, who shared a similar mission. The Catechesis of the Good Shepherd community—frequently mentioned in the pages that follow—will want to take special note of what Skublics has accomplished here, as it may be a resource in trying to share with adults the rich theology that undergirds its work with children.

In her essay about the sources that most influenced her own thinking, Sofia Cavalletti says of one scholar, "I am generally diffident about theologians, considering they complicate matters. This definitely is not the case [here]. Despite the lofty level and the great quantity of his writing, his ideas are extremely clear and he expounds them clearly. Once I began reading his works, I went on devouring them." I do believe Cavalletti would speak similarly of this work.

It takes a long, long time to speak with the clarity and joy of the young.

Ann Garrido
Associate Professor
Aquinas Institute of Theology

CHAPTER 1

Plunged into the Trinity

*The Significance of the Trinitarian Content
of our Baptismal Faith*

*Our Primary Encounter with Father, Son, and Holy Spirit:
What do the Words and Actions Say?*

LET ME BEGIN IN the name of the Father, and of the Son, and of the Holy Spirit, as we begin all our prayers, and all the significant things we do as Christians, even though we often do this quite unconsciously, by habit, out of routine, seldom really thinking about the fact that our whole Christian existence is rooted in this Trinitarian origin. In fact, I have heard more than enough sermons on occasions like Trinity Sunday suggesting that the Mystery of the Trinity is something theologians worry about but is really not for ordinary faithful to try to understand.

Yet, our very being is rooted in the Trinity, and patterned by the Trinity. At the beginning, we are baptized in the name of the Trinity, every time we turn to God we start in the name of the Trinity, all of our liturgies are structured in an explicitly Trinitarian fashion, and our basic formula of articulating our faith, the creed, is divided into three parts to speak about the three divine Persons. There must be some extremely important, primary, and fundamental significance to this Reality, this character, this unique nature of God, our origin and destination, who has created and shaped all things, and especially us, after his own image and likeness. There must be some vital consequences for us to the fact that all our being is oriented to and shaped by the Trinity.

And that is why I thought that we could do no better than exploring this fundamental and yet neglected or misunderstood aspect of our faith and our very being.

Now I entitled this book, and its opening essay *Plunged into the Trinity,* because, quite literally, that is where the whole story begins for us, when we are plunged—with the Greek word, *"baptized"*—into the Trinity.

And because it is that liturgy of Baptism, that plunging, that expresses, realizes, and starts us in our new existence, and because that liturgy is really our first and primary encounter with God and the source of all of our subsequent growth into and understanding of our Christian existence and everything we get to know and believe about it, it makes sense that we should begin by examining what really, actually happens in that ritual: what do the words really say is happening, and what happens as we are plunged, immersed, baptized into that water, being told that in fact we are being plunged, baptized into the name of the Father and of the Son and of the Holy Spirit?

The Words and the Ritual: What They Really Say

I want to highlight some interesting things about this whole operation of trying to decipher and understand what really happens. This is really the nature of theology that we are going to be engaged in: theology being the effort to interpret and understand what has really happened to us in that liturgical encounter when we first met God in a real formative way. It can be truly said that the experience of our becoming our new reality through this liturgical encounter is itself our primary knowledge of God: primary theology. The effort of sitting down *after* what has happened in that first encounter and trying to understand it and to make sense out of this primary knowledge is simply secondary and derivative.[1]

So, we are all "theologians" the moment we have encountered God in Word and Sacrament and proceeded to try to understand what has happened. And of course since that activity by its very nature leads us more intimately to be face-to-face with God, one of the early Fathers of the Church could rightly say that anybody who can truly pray is a theologian!

Another way of saying this is that: *digesting* the liturgy in a reflective, contemplative silence, extending, cherishing, and savoring that encounter is the real, existential role of theology. So, we must not write off theology as some sort of a rarefied hobby for odd-ball specialists who have nothing to do with real life. *Real* theology is *our life,* our prayer, our learning to understand who we are, what we are here for and where we are going: our intelligent cultivation of our relationship with God.

So, then, let us look at what these words and rituals of our liturgies, and specifically those of Baptism, actually say and do.

Now both *words* and *rituals* are *symbols.* So we need to understand how symbols work. And it is better to think about symbols as something *happening,* rather than as of some static objects: an image, for example. It *can* be an image or an object as well, but, inasmuch as, for the observer or participant, two realms, two realities come together in that symbol, something is *happening.* And it is that *happening* that constitutes the symbol. *Syn-ballein* in Greek means something like *dancing together,* we might even say *dancing or jumping into each other, co-in-ciding.* And that is how a symbol becomes an event of revelation.

Symbols, by belonging to two different realms simultaneously and bringing those two together in one reality that can be seen, heard, touched, done, performed, actually reveal and realize something for us *by that connection* that would otherwise

---

1. This state of affairs is illustrated by the early Church's practice of baptizing even adults after only partial introduction to the faith, giving them the creed at their Baptism and following their initiation with post-baptismal catechesis, leading them to understand and digest what had happened to them.

remain hidden, undiscovered. Carl Gustav Jung, the great Swiss psychologist of the last century, explained that symbols connect some known, visible, tangible reality—like being plunged into water—with something we do *not* know, something that may be hidden, submerged in our unconscious. And, because of that connection, the unknown reality, that may in fact be an essential aspect of our self, is revealed, brought to the surface. And so, for Jung, symbols are powerful means in our growing self-realization, our self-integration, our becoming more fully who we are.

I guess you can see why symbols then are the perfect natural realities to become sacramental vehicles for God's hidden activity for us. It is because of this natural function of symbols, symbolic expressions, words, actions, rituals, that these things are so perfectly suited to become sacraments that communicate the hidden gifts of grace from God.

We can therefore also think of words and rituals as *media of communication,* all of them addressing one or more of our senses: sight, hearing, touching, tasting, even smelling, communicating to us in an embodied fashion, adapted to our human nature and condition, the otherwise unheard message or intangible gift of God. Hence the verbal/ritual *embodiment* of God's communication with us.

In fact, the very foundation of this communication between God and us is the Incarnation: God becoming man, divine Word becoming human word through Jesus, divine touch human touch, divine love human love. Jesus is the primary, Fundamental Sacrament, *the* sacrament of our encounter with God. In and through him we meet God himself in his humanity, hear God himself speaking like a man, receive God himself. And that is what all the sacraments do as extensions of the incarnate Jesus, who is present and acting in and through them.

Think of this Fundamental Sacrament extending himself into bread and wine to enter into our very physical being to be united with us, and making us into himself!

Well now, let us finally apply all this to Baptism. Both from the study of depth psychology and from the comparative study of various cultures and religions, it emerges that water has a universal, archetypal-symbolic meaning. It is obviously *the* primordial element, a primordial source of life. There are apparently similar origins-of-the-world myths to our own creation narrative, describing the emergence of the created world out of water, water being the first and as yet undefined, shapeless, primordial matter, out of which specific, concrete creatures are formed.

The biblical account of the Flood presents God as returning his spoiled creation, as it were, to the primordial element and again bringing it forth anew. The chosen People of the Old Testament are really born out of being brought through the Red Sea to their new life and identity. Very similarly we ourselves begin our life in the waters of the maternal womb, and water remains the most important element to sustain our life. So water has a strong symbolic meaning for us, to do with life. There are initiation and purification rituals in other religions as well that consist of having a person submerged in water and brought out to newness of life.

Hence baptism—an untranslated Greek word—simply meaning submerging, plunging, which of course was the original form of Baptism. So, without any words of explanation, the symbolic *rite itself* suggests that what we are trying to replicate, enact, experience, in a physical way, is a plunge into the origins of life, and then coming out of the waters of the womb of the baptismal font to a new life.

But then we have to examine what is being *said* by the Word accompanying this gesture. The priest says as he dunks, or drenches the candidate three times: I baptize you in the name of the Father, and of the Son, and of the Holy Spirit.

Now that is meant to be the exact rendering of the account of Jesus' mandate in Matthew 28:19. So, let us look at that original text a little closer: what is it *actually* saying?

Matthew is reporting the words of Jesus in Greek: "All authority (or power) in heaven and on earth has been given to me.

Go therefore and *make disciples* of all nations, (by) *baptizing* them *in* the *name* of the Father and of the Son and of the Holy Spirit." So, disciples are made by being baptized. I want to look more closely at these three words or phrases: *baptizing, in,* and *in the name of.*

As already mentioned, baptizing simply means dunking, immersing, submerging, plunging. And as this is said, the candidate is actually plunged into *water.* But what is *said* is not that he is plunged into *water,* but really into *something else.* And this brings me to the next word to be examined: baptizing *in* . . .

Now the way this is commonly translated seems to suggest that we are doing something, baptizing, *under the auspices of, on behalf of, in the name of somebody,* namely the Trinity. But is that what the text really says? Let us just go to Matthew's original. I'm afraid that is Greek. As we shall see in a minute, the fact that Matthew was a *Jew* is very significant, but he is writing in *Greek.* And what he is quoting Jesus as having said is, "make disciples of all nations, (by) baptizing (immersing) them *into* the name . . . (*eis to onoma*), not *en to onoma,* which would mean "*in* the name."

Well, what do we make of that? It does not make sense: plunging somebody into a *name!*

And here is where Matthew's *Jewishness* comes into the picture, and maybe even *Jesus'* Jewishness. And Jesus of course had spoken Aramaic, a form of Hebrew. And Jews considered it unacceptable arrogance to even *speak about* God directly: they would typically refer to the *name* of Yahweh, the *name* of the Lord, or the *name* of God.

Well then, let us take this insight back to the text, and see what Matthew, or Jesus, is *really saying:* "All authority (or power) in heaven and on earth has been given to me. Go therefore and *make disciples* of all nations, by means of plunging them into (really) the Father, and the Son, and the Holy Spirit."

And this is why I entitled our investigations *Plunged into the Trinity.* In the following, we will try to unpack this mind-blowing sentence somewhat, obviously not being able to do much more than skimming the surface—the rest being our meditation for a lifetime.

Through Jesus into the Trinity

We get some help from the other very important text on Baptism, in Romans 6:3-4, where Paul tells us, with the very same Greek word, that we have been baptized, immersed, plunged, *into* Christ Jesus, *into* his death, being *"con-buried"* with him, so that we can rise to his new life with him, through him, in him. And, of course, that is how the body of Christ, "the whole Christ," the Church, is born, by us being incorporated into the second Person of the Trinity. In and through him then, we are brought into the Communion of the Trinity. That is what sharing the life of God by grace means.

CHAPTER 2

Sacramental Realism and the Plunge

The Pattern of Sacramentality

WE LIVE IN A supposedly sophisticated age, where things unseen and not subject to immediate experience or scientific experiment are called into question. When the first manned Russian space-craft—called Sputnik—returned to earth, its pilot, Yuri Gagarin, declared that he had been up in the skies and could not see God, or any evidence for God, anywhere. The Soviets made hay out of this "obvious proof" that God did not exist. More recently, and applying more pseudo-science to the problem, the likes of Oxford professor Richard Dawkins have argued that the essentially tangible universe does not require an invisible God to explain it.

In fact, the *invisibility* and *inaccessibility*—from our point of view—of the Divine, of the Reality that is much more self-sufficient, independent, and enduring and absolute than our visibly evolving universe, had been recognized long before these supposedly sophisticated clever-clogs came along. It is simple and consistent biblical teaching that "No one has ever seen God," and that—but for some special arrangements making a meeting of visible and invisible possible—no one can go to God, reach God, discover God, enter into any kind of relationship with God. And this is so because God is of a *different order of being*—in fact, he is not even in any sense of an "order of being," as beings go: he is not *one* being at all, but in fact the *source* of being, Being itself.

For created, particularly material things, their *being* is a *derivative* reality, caused by something else, something beyond them, that *made* them *be*. However far we stretch our imagination of a chain of causality, somewhere we need to acknowledge the ultimate, absolute, and uncaused foundation, source, explanation of all being . . . At the very least, that much we know about God. But that is not *knowing,* having *met,* or personally *relating to* God . . . There is no way for a human to *directly* relate to God or *experience* God.

And the Christian story gives us *God's own solution* to this problem. As we understand it, God has in fact created us *to be in relationship* with him. God himself *is* the ultimate *relationship.* His nature is Trinity in unity. And the whole point of creation appears to be for God to *expand his relationality,* his divine communion and community, beyond himself. In the medieval language of St. Thomas Aquinas, God is by definition *the Supreme Good,* which means love itself (another word for relationship), and the nature of the good, of love, of relating, is that it is *diffusivum sui.* By nature, it tends to pour itself out, give itself, communicate itself, spread itself.

Now, again, the biblical account presents an original state of harmony, where God, man-and-woman, and all the created universe were in harmonious unity, transparent to each other. How that could be explained we do not know, because that experience was shattered by the divisive action of human beings, becoming autonomous and separate from God.

To make a long story short, the ingenious plan and design was that God would himself *step into his creation*—without ceasing to be God, he would also *become creation:* human, take on himself our nature, and thus create a *bridge* over the gap. And so we have the *Mystery of the Incarnation,* which becomes the *Fundamental*

Sacrament of our communion with the otherwise completely[1] inaccessible God.

Now I have introduced the critical word *mystery*. And it is this key word that is particularly rooted in the Epistle to the Ephesians, where we are introduced to the *grand design, plan, economy* of God, existing in his mind from all eternity, all summed up in this wonderful word, *mystery*. The Mystery of God is his *structure*, his *economy*, his great way of *realizing the relationship of communion* with us humans, for which he had created us.

Now as the epistle describes this Mystery, it unfolds in *successive stages*. Originally it is with God, in inaccessible light, from all eternity, as a plan, a design, a reality to be implemented "in the fullness of time" (1). And then, in the process of his covenanted relationship with his chosen people, it is gradually unfolded, realized, implemented over time, through what we call "the history of salvation" (2).

In its final stage "the Mystery" is realized, embodied, in the marriage of God with humanity, in the flesh and Person of Jesus, true man and true God in one and the same Person (3). And so we speak of the *Mystery of Christ*—not in the sense of there being some incomprehensible *secret* about Christ, but in the sense in which Christ himself *is* the Mystery—the embodiment, the visible, human realization and implementation of God's Mystery: his eternal plan. In fact, it is an *essential* element to the biblical notion of *mystery*, that it *is revealed* and made accessible, so as to afford us a tangible connection to God himself.

And so, in the native language of the early Church, Greek, this word, *mysterion* was carried on and transferred to the *extension of the Incarnation*, the Body of Christ, the Church, and all those instances when the Church extends itself to us, embodying us into the incarnate God himself. And so, we speak of the *Mystery of the Church*, the *Mystery of Baptism*, the *Mystery of the Eucharist*, indeed, to this day, in Greek, the word we in the West have translated as *sacrament*, continues to be *mysterion, mystery* (4).

---

1. See Eph 1:3–14.

And so we understand that mystery—or sacrament—is a visible, tangible *experience* of the divine, *a way of touching God,* a way of sharing in his uncreated being and life, his love, his grace, his absolute immortality, a way of being mysteriously embraced into his triune being.

This means a certain *translation* or *transposition* of a divine, inaccessible Reality, into a humanly understood experience. God, who has no hands, has to touch us with human hands. God, who has no physical voice, has to speak to us through the human word. And so we come to these symbolic actions that mean something to us, psychologically, emotionally, associating the divine happening that we cannot see with the human happening that we *do* experience.

And so it was that the *dying to the old man,* to our *old existence* and *separate identity, dying into the death of Christ,* so we can share in it, in his burial, and so also in his Resurrection, was experienced by acting out a stripping away of the old *persona,* by being stripped naked, and then by drowning and a burial, being plunged down into water, symbolizing—and experiencing—a certain annihilation. And then, on the other side, the new Christian would emerge, symbolizing—and experiencing—a new birth, a rising into a new life. And the fact that this was the very life of Christ was symbolized by the new Christian being vested in a new white garment, and given a lighted candle, the light of Christ. So, sacrament (or "mystery") is an experience of the ineffable divine Reality in which we come to participate through this visible, tangible rite.

Initiation: The Plunge and Anointing of the Paschal Sacrament

So, what we see and hear and experience is the *physical embodiment of something happening that we could otherwise not perceive.* There is an old principle that we can find out what the Church *understands and believes* by looking at what she *does,* liturgically. We can read it out of the rite.

And so it is with Christian initiation. As we have seen in the first chapter, there are two principal biblical texts that tell us what happens. Paul in his Epistle to the Romans (6:3–11) actually describes the rite and its meaning. We have been "immersed into" the death of Christ and buried with him, so we are raised, with him and in him, to his new life, which, essentially, is beyond death and beyond the reach of death. We have analyzed this text in the first chapter.

The other text we have also looked at in chapter 1 (Matt 28:18–20) is a report of Jesus' own words, before his ascension, instructing his disciples about their job, giving them their "missionary mandate."

Now in the Marcan version of this "missionary mandate"— which is the earlier one—Jesus is supposed to have added: "Whoever believes and is baptized will be saved; he who does not . . . will be condemned" (Mark 16:16).

So we can see that the whole business of "salvation" is about being *incorporated into the Body of Christ* (the "Mystery of Christ"), the Church, and through that into the Communion, being and life of the Holy Trinity—being restored to—in fact a higher than the original degree of union with God.

And *because* the mystery into which we are plunged is essentially the *Paschal Mystery*—of Jesus dying and rising to restore our communion—Baptism was normatively celebrated *in the center of the Easter liturgy,* as is provided for in the Easter Vigil rite even today, acting out the entire process of initiation: hearing the Word and receiving the faith, being baptized and anointed, and fully joining the Church in the Eucharist by First Communion.

What about *Confirmation or Chrismation?* Anointing with fragrant oil is the ancient rite of making prophets, priests, and kings. It symbolizes—among other things—*spiritual empowerment* by God. The Holy Spirit is referred to in traditional hymnody as "the soul's anointing from above." In fact, the title Christ—*Christos*—means precisely: the Anointed One, the One on whom the Spirit has descended. Now having become identified with Christ

13

through Baptism, we have come to share in his function as priest, prophet, and king, and so, from earliest times, there followed a *post-baptismal anointing*, like a rub-down with lotion after a bath, to complete the symbolism of the rite, and to show that we have been *ordained into Christ* by receiving his Spirit.

It is difficult to ascribe a radically *distinct* function and grace to the sacrament of Confirmation, as it was originally never separated from Baptism, but was an integral part of it, and Baptism itself confers the gift of the Holy Spirit. In fact, it is interesting to note that, in the later Western Rite, when Confirmation was routinely delayed and celebrated separately, a post-baptismal anointing remained, with the same gesture and words as the now separated Confirmation rite had.

Why did Confirmation become separated and delayed? We have to blame the bishops for that. Originally, and in principle still, the bishop, being the head of the local church, is the minister of initiation: it is his function to integrate a new convert into the community of the Body of Christ. In the early Church in Asia Minor every local town or village had one church, and its pastor was the bishop. Eventually, as the Christian population grew, deacons and priests multiplied to assist the bishop and were delegated to perform some of the bishop's functions. Still, today, priests baptize and preside over the eucharist *on behalf* of the bishop, by his delegated authority.

And so, when bishops were no longer easily available for every Baptism, there were *two alternative solutions* found, one predominantly in the East, the other predominantly in the West. In the East the bishop *delegated the entire initiation* to the priest. The bishop consecrated the oil of chrism and the priest used this chrism to confirm the neophyte, immediately after the Baptism, and admit him to communion within the same service. So the bishop was in a sense "present" through the chrism he had consecrated. This way, the three-part initiation rite remained integrated in the Eastern church where, even if a *baby* is baptized, it is immediately confirmed/chrismated and communicated.

In the West, on the other hand, the bishops reserved the function of Confirmation to themselves, and so, of course, this completing act had to be deferred until the bishop could come in person.

While many more or less speculative meanings have been attached to this separated rite of Confirmation in the West, one very significant point has to do with the bishop's dual role of being both the head of the local church *and* its link to the universal Church through his communion with the other bishops of local churches. In this dual role the bishop symbolizes the fact that a person initiated into the local church by a local pastor is then "confirmed" to have been received in the universal Church by the same token, and can receive communion in all local churches that are in communion with each other. In the mathematics of ecclesiology, each local church is sacramentally identical with every other local church, and, indeed, with the Communion of all the local churches, which makes up the universal Church.

And, of course, the initiation is complete when the new Christian has received the Body and Blood of Christ in holy Communion.

CHAPTER 3

The Covenantal Dynamic
of the Eucharist

IN THIS CHAPTER I would like to reflect on the theme of *the Eucharist,
particularly in its ecclesiological significance: the Eucharist, as it is
the heart of the Church, as, indeed, in a sense it is the Church itself
in becoming. It is the activity (the action, the verb) that becomes the
reality (the thing, the noun).* To say that "the Eucharist makes the
Church" means that our action, sacramentally realizing the action
of Christ here and now, our *doing* the Eucharist, makes us into
being the Church.

For those Christians accustomed to referring to the eucharistic action as "communion," this can be formulated as *doing* communion makes us *become* and *be* communion: the Communion
that is the Church. What we *do* is what we *become.* To paraphrase
one key sentence that occurs in both foundational documents of
the Second Vatican Council, the one on the Liturgy and the first
one on the Church: the very *being* of the Church is derived from
the Eucharist and is completed and fulfilled in the Eucharist. Or:
the Church is most completely and perfectly being herself in the
act of offering the Eucharist.

On one level this fact is so obvious and simple that you
can sum it up in one sentence and go home, saying: I've always
known that. God becomes man; *that* man becomes bread; we eat

and assimilate that bread into ourselves, and so we *become* that one bread, that one body, that one man: *the whole Christ.* And so, that one man has become the many, and the many have become the one, the one that returns to the Father, through his sacrifice, as the many, into the Communion of the Three. We have *become communion* with Christ, through whom we come to share in the Communion of the Trinity. Period. God's entire *opus* completed. Yes, of course it will become *manifest* in the parousia, in our visible resurrection, but, essentially, it has already been accomplished.

And yet, of course this huge and complex mystery has so many ramifications and implications that we can not only spend a weekend thinking about it, but we can construct an entire four-year graduate theology curriculum upon it.

But we want to teach little children, as early as possible, what this great Mystery of the Mass is, so they can get the maximum benefit from participating in it. How do we tell them what the Mass is?

When I was a child, we had to learn a lot of confusing things about the Mass. It was a *sacrifice.* But it was also a *meal.* It was a *memorial.* But it was also the *real presence of Christ.* It was *thanksgiving* and also *petition* and *intercession.* A lot of things to remember, and it was all the more difficult to remember them because we didn't quite understand the *connections, the whys and hows, the necessary unity and logic* of all that was happening.

And yet, if we only look into the *words and action* of the liturgy, it should all come together beautifully. This incidentally is a general principle for theology: for theology is the systematic reflection on and articulation and understanding of the Christian experience of becoming what we are, chiefly through the liturgy of Word and Sacrament, bringing that great Mystery into our presence, so we can enter into it. So we need to *read our theology out of the liturgy,* primarily. That's what it means that *"lex orandi est lex credendi."* In fact, it has been said that the liturgy *is* the *primary theology,* the primary, experiential encounter and way of knowing and articulating. What we reflectively draw out of this experience and conceptualize, that is *secondary, derivative* theology. So let us look at the liturgy.

We know that the Mass, the Eucharist, was instituted at the Last Supper. It was when Jesus, having gone through a few ritual gestures and words, broadly following the rites of the traditional Passover supper, said to his disciples: "Do *this* as my *memorial.*"

So, all we have to do is ask: what was that *"this"* that Jesus was doing or had done, and what did he mean by us doing *that* "as [his] *memorial*"?

First of all, what was he, or had he been doing?

Now there is some scholarly debate about whether or not the Last Supper was an actual *Passover* meal. There is a bit of inconsistency between the biblical accounts: one text explicitly stating that it *was* a Passover meal, but the other, by dating it a day before the Jewish Passover, would seem to suggest that it was a *chaburah* meal. The dilemma is not terribly significant, because the *chaburah* meal essentially followed the same outline and modeled the same memorial theology as the Passover meal, only it was a weekly affair, rather than the once-yearly solemn memorial of the Exodus. Personally, I believe the argument for it *having been* a Passover meal, as is explicitly claimed by the Synoptic Gospels, is a bit stronger than the argument against, but, as I said, the argument is of no substantial significance.

In any case, this ritual meal was in fact a *liturgical* act, rooted in the Covenant, which it was supposed to renew, revive, remember, and make present and operative. It was in effect a *memorial celebration of the Covenant,* the Covenant in which a special relationship and mutual commitment between God and his people had been established. The meal was simply a *ritual enactment* of that founding moment, when the Jews were freed, redeemed out of Egypt. It was a *thanking-and-praising memorial* which, remembering God's covenantal blessings on his people, gave God thanks and praise, asking him to *also remember* and renew and continue his blessings on his covenantal people.

So, there are *two key words* that sum up the entire meaning and action of this rite that Jesus performed with his Apostles and refocused that night on *his own* fulfilling and renewing that Covenant: the Hebrew words BRK and ZKR—*blessing* and *remembering*.

Both of these words in this case denote a *mutual* blessing and remembering. This was a *"mirabile commercium"*—a marvelous exchange—between God and humanity, God and his people, the community he had created for himself in and through that Covenant, in which he said: "I am going to be *your God* and you are going to be *my people*." And God made special promises to his people, committed himself to take special care of them. And he also required of *them* some special commitments, giving them the Commandments, so that God's and his people's *mutual fidelity* to that *Bund,* that bond of the Covenant would continue in perpetuity.

And to keep this covenant relationship going, God especially required of the people that they must *remember*—both ritually and spiritually—the Covenant in fidelity. For, as he said: "Wherever I have (= cause, choose to have) my name remembered, I will come to you and bless you" (Exod 20:24).

Now this *solemn and formal institution of the Covenant,* described in chapters 19 to 24 of Exodus, is a sort of focal *point in the history of God's dealings with his people, which is really the entire old Covenant history of salvation,* aptly described as a presentation of God's *developing relationship* with his people, starting in the very Garden of Eden, suggested in the deluge story, becoming quite explicit with Abraham, Isaac and Jacob, then Moses, the Exodus, and finally formally ritualized at Sinai. It is this Covenant history that Jesus *completes* and *claims as his own,* to be memorialized in the Eucharist. We need to understand this special relationship, formalized here, as one of *mutual fidelity* to *mutual promises and commitments* made between God and his people.

And this is where the concept of mutual *remembrance* comes in. When God declared that "Wherever I choose to have my name remembered, I will come to you and bless you," this is both a reference to the ritual memorials the people celebrate as part of their keeping the Covenant present and alive, and also a statement to the effect that, there God *himself* will remember and therefore "come to you and bless you."

This notion of remembrance or memorial is rooted in the Hebrew biblical understanding that when God remembers it is not just some idle mental recollection, as it were, but his remembering means *action*. When God remembers someone that means he comes and blesses them. Or, if he remembers someone's sins, that means he visits and punishes them, and when he remembers someone's sins no more, that means those sins no longer exist: they are forgiven, wiped out. God's *remembering* is what *keeps things in being* by his blessing, creating, maintaining, growing. Or, on the other hand, he keeps unforgiven sins in being by remembering them.

Another feature of the Hebrew word for *remembering* is that it is identical with *reminding,* and this linguistic feature carries the theology of *mutuality* in these memorials: God remembers his people and "chooses"—i.e., causes—them to remember him, and when the people remember God and his Covenant, with its promises, by the same token they "remind" God, and so cause him to remember again and renew his blessings.

This is both a *ritual/sacramental* remembrance that underlies and explains the real presence of Christ in the Eucharist, and a *spiritual* culture that brings us into and keeps us in the presence of God and our covenantal relationship with him, through our sustained mindfulness—the biblical "praying always" or "praying without ceasing," which, from the Desert Fathers on, was cultivated as a means of living in the presence of God.

So, a simple illustration of this mutual remembering/reminding dialectic would be:

So, what Jesus was doing at the Last Supper, celebrating the Memorial of the Passover, was retelling, and thus bringing into the present, as well as reenacting, the covenantal blessings of the Passover sacrifice of the lamb and its ritual consumption, followed by the Exodus or rescue of his people from Egypt. So, the recalling and reenacting of that past covenantal blessing brought it into the present. And then the celebrating community explicitly "reminded" God to renew these blessings in the present.

But then Jesus said: "Do this—keep doing this—as *my* memorial," echoing—for the *new* Covenant—what God had commanded the people of the *old* Covenant, ordering them to celebrate the memorial: remembering his name, so he could come to them and bless them.

And so this brings us to the *other* key word for understanding the eucharist: BRK or *blessing*.

Once again, blessing is also a *bi-directional* word for a mutual action: God has blessed his people, and his people bless God. The *same* word is used to express *both* actions. And then the dialectic continues by God renewing his blessing in response, and the people once again blessing *God* in response, and so it goes: the covenant of mutual blessings is kept alive and moving.

Of course, though the *same* word is used for both actors and actions, we realize that when *God* blesses that is something different from when a *human* blesses. For God, blessing is an outgoing divine action, somewhat synonymous with creation: God gives . . . everything from being, life, and every enhancement of being and life. The human, on the other hand, acknowledges gratefully God's blessings and blesses, that is, praises, thanks, and glorifies him for it. Hence the word *eucharist*: the Greek translation for the Hebrew BRK or "blessing."

This dialectic too can be illustrated with the same circle:

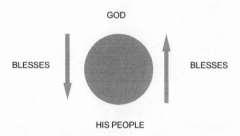

GOD

BLESSES   BLESSES

HIS PEOPLE

And so, now, we can look at the central text and action of the Eucharist, and see how these two key words come together and tell us exactly what happens.

Eucharistic Prayer 2 of the Roman Rite[1]

It is truly right and just, our duty and salvation,

always and everywhere to *give you thanks,* Father most holy, through your beloved Son, Jesus Christ, your Word,	eucharistia/berekah
through whom *you made all things,* whom you sent to us as Savior and Redeemer, incarnate by the Holy Spirit and born of the Virgin. Fulfilling your will and gaining for you a holy people, he stretched out his hands as he suffered, to break the bonds of death and show forth the resurrection.	anamnesis/ memorial narrative=preface

1. www.liturgyoffice.org.uk/Missal.

Therefore, with the Angels and all the Saints we
proclaim your glory,
as with one voice we say:

Holy, Holy, Holy is the Lord God of hosts.   (insert resuming
Heaven and earth are full of your glory.   thanks-and-praise)
Hosanna in the highest.
Blessed is he who comes
in the name of the Lord.
Hosanna in the highest.
You are indeed the Holy One, O Lord,
you are the wellspring of all holiness.

Therefore, *make holy these gifts,* we pray,   consecratory
by the dew of your Spirit,   epiclesis
that they may become for us
the Body + and Blood of our Lord,
Jesus Christ.

Who, as he *was handed over*   anamnesis/
and entered willingly into his Passion,   memorial
took bread and, giving thanks, broke it,   narrative continues
and gave it to his disciples, saying:
Take this, all of you, and eat of it,
for this is my Body,
which will be given up for you.
In the same way, when supper was ended,
he took the chalice
and, once more giving you thanks,
he gave it to his disciples, saying:
Take this, all of you and drink from it,
for this is the Cup of my Blood,
the Blood of the new and eternal Covenant;
it will be poured out for you and for all
for the forgiveness of sins.
Do this in memory of me.

The mystery of faith.
We proclaim your death, O Lord,
and profess your Resurrection
until you come in glory.
or—
When we eat this Bread and drink this Cup,
we proclaim your death, O Lord,
until you come again.
or—
Savior of the world, save us,
for by your cross and Resurrection
you have set us free.

memorial acclama-
tion followed by:

Therefore, as we *celebrate the memorial*
of his death and Resurrection,
we offer you, Lord,
the Bread of life and the Chalice of salvation, giving
thanks that you have deemed us worthy to stand in
your presence and serve you.

memorial prayer:
anamnesis

Humbly *we pray*
that, *sharing in the Body and Blood of Christ,*
we may be *gathered into one*
by the Holy Spirit.
Remember, Lord, your Church spread throughout
the world,
and bring her to the fullness of charity, together
with N. our Pope and N. our Bishop and all the
clergy.

communion
epiclesis
expanded by:

Remember also our brothers and sisters
who have fallen asleep in the hope of the
resurrection,
and all who have died in your mercy:
welcome them into the light of your countenance.
Have mercy on us all, we pray,
that with the blessed Virgin Mary, Mother of God,
the blessed Apostles,
and all the Saints from every age who have pleased
you,
we may be worthy to share eternal life,
and may praise and glorify you
through your Son, Jesus Christ.

intercessions

Through him, and with him, and in him,
to you, O God, almighty Father,
in the unity of the Holy Spirit,
is *all honor and glory,*
for ever and ever.
Amen.

*doxology resuming
thanks and praise=
eucharist/berakah*

Now a word about this very important prayer, the *epiclesis.*
I understand that the Catechesis of the Good Shepherd makes a
special effort to explain to the children this invocation, calling
down the Holy Spirit, both on the offerings and on the people. In
our developed eucharistic prayers in fact we have *two epicleses,* as
you have seen: first for the consecration of the elements of bread
and wine, and later for fruitful communion, that through receiving
the consecrated elements, the people themselves may be consecrated into the one Body by the Holy Spirit.

It is instructive to look at the very *oldest* extant eucharistic
prayer, the one of Hippolytus' *Apostolic Tradition,* from which
our prayer is derived:[2] It only has *one single epiclesis,* which brings
out the very thing we are talking about, that *the Eucharist makes
the Church:* that the consecration of the bread and wine has as its
very purpose the consecration of the people who receive it into

2. https://en.wikipedia.org/wiki/Anaphora_of_the_Apostolic_Tradition;
Botte, *La Tradition Apostolique,* 13–14.

the Body of Christ. Here is the text, immediately following on the Institution Account:

> And we pray that you would *send your Holy Spirit*
> to the *oblation* of your Holy Church.
> In their *gathering together,*
> give to all those who *partake* of your holy mysteries
> *the fullness of the Holy Spirit,*
> toward the strengthening of the faith in truth,
> that we may praise you and glorify you,
> through your son Jesus Christ.

And so we return to our circle illustrating the covenantal dynamic dialectically moving the relationship between God and people forward, to see how the two key concepts of blessing and memorial are integrated in one movement.

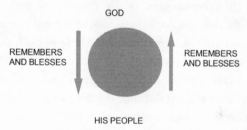

GOD

REMEMBERS AND BLESSES   REMEMBERS AND BLESSES

HIS PEOPLE

And so we see that this cycle of mutual remembering and blessing is *the dynamism that moves the Covenant life of the covenanted people forward* in mutual fidelity, faithfulness, observance.

So, when we revisit the institution of the Eucharist, we see how Jesus has built into the traditional Jewish liturgical framework of the Covenant remembrance and praise over the Passover supper his own covenantal memorial praise, or "eucharist," telling his Apostles to "do this as my memorial," until he comes again.

Now, what about *the ritual action,* the breaking and sharing of the bread and the drinking of the cup?

The *words* and the *rite* of course *mutually interpret* each other. And so, the breaking and sharing of the bread, consecrated into the Body of the new victim, Christ—representing both the killing and eating of the paschal lamb and the communion-sacrifice of the bullock at Sinai—and the wine consecrated into the sacrificial Blood of Christ, representing both the blood smeared onto the door posts of the houses in Egypt and the bullock's blood at Sinai —memorialize both the Passover of the Exodus and the ritual at Sinai, sealing the bond of the Covenant.

The reader will remember that at Sinai a circle of twelve stones was erected, representing the community of the twelve tribes of Israel, with one stone in the center, representing God. Then they offered "bullocks for Yahweh as *communion sacrifices*," and half of the sacrificial animal's blood was sprinkled on the central stone, the other half on the people—or perhaps the twelve stones representing the people.

Communion sacrifices were essentially *Covenant* rites, symbolizing the "communion" of the community with their God, through sharing the same meal. So, *sacrificing* the animal and dividing it wasn't just *giving up* something to God, as an end in itself: it was preparing a communion meal to be shared with God. And so was the sprinkling of the life-giving blood on both parties a symbol of their sharing the same life. So, *sacrifice and communion meal are not two independent meanings but two aspects of the same uniting ritual.* And, of course, all in the circle, uniting with God, thereby also become a unity among themselves. So, *the Eucharist,* first sealing and then reenacting the Covenant, *makes the Church.* But it doesn't do so without the "thanking-and-praising memorial" prayer, which, again, is not *yet another* separate function but rather the dynamic of bringing the communion-sacrifice into the present.

And that is how the Eucharist continues the dynamic of God the Father remembering his people and his Covenant with them, and blessing them again and again, "wherever he chooses his name to be remembered" by his people in this way, and his people remembering, memorializing their Covenant, through this observance, are built into the community, made into the communion of the Church through the Eucharist, to the praise and glory of God, the whole dialectical process to be fulfilled and completed on the Last Day.

CHAPTER 4

The Eucharist Makes the Church

THE EUCHARIST IS THE heart of the Church; indeed, in a sense, it *is* the Church itself in becoming.

This huge and complex Mystery has so many ramifications and implications that we can not only spend a couple of hours thinking about it, but we can construct an entire four-year graduate theology curriculum upon it. Which is precisely what we did at Mount Angel Seminary when I was serving there as academic dean. And it was through this process of redesigning the whole theological curriculum that I came to know Fr. (now Monsignor) Paul McPartlan (who was introduced to leaders of the Catechesis of the Good Shepherd by Sophia Cavalletti) through the article "The Eucharist Makes the Church," which is the theme of this chapter. This is incidentally the title of one of McPartlan's books, a classic I recommend you to read.

More specifically I discovered Paul McPartlan through work I was doing on the rapprochement between Eastern Orthodoxy and the Catholic Church, because Paul was working on the same subject at the same time, and it was in particular through the meeting of the minds of the Orthodox theologian John Zizioulas and the Catholic theologian Henri de Lubac that this rapprochement could be most vividly followed, and it was through this rapprochement that the features of a "eucharistic ecclesiology" most clearly reemerged. Paul compared these two thinkers in his magnificent book, and I invited him on two separate occasions to be our speaker for the annual theological symposium of the Seminary.

Now our subject, *the Eucharist actually producing the Church,* or rather, the *retrieval* of this ancient emphasis, of the Eucharist producing the Church, over a little more than a century, has had a great deal to do with the Orthodox Eastern Churches and the Western Catholic Church coming ever so close to restoring their original union. So, I'd like to pull into relief a few moments from the *history* of this recovery.

Paul McPartlan likes to quote de Lubac saying that, roughly through the *first* millennium of the Church, this understanding, that the Church emerges from, and is generated by, the Eucharist, the celebration of the Mass, as rendering the work of Christ present in summary form, was taken for granted. And, in this, East and West had a common *sacramental* vision of the Church, as the *sacramental product* of celebrating and reenacting the work of Christ in the Eucharist.

But then, through the *second* millennium, partly as a result of the estrangement of East and West, with their respective mentalities, and the gradual ascendancy of Roman juridicism, the Western church increasingly saw itself as an "institution," something founded by Christ, much as an organization with a legal charter may be founded by someone, for the purpose of performing certain activities, in the case of the Church these being the communication of the saving mysteries of Christ to people, such as, most importantly, through the offering of Christ's sacrifice in the Eucharist and making participation in him possible through Holy Communion. So, more and more people understood *the Church as making the Eucharist,* consecrating, offering and distributing. We had to have the Church, for without her we couldn't have the Eucharist, we couldn't have Christ.

True enough, but one unfortunate side effect of this one-sided way of viewing the Church was that her very existence came to be seen as being rooted in a sort of juridical action, and all power, authority, and enablement in the Church came to be seen as being due to this legal act of Jesus founding, instituting, and empowering the Church, rather than to the sacramental presence of his reconciling sacrifice.

Apart from this view being able to create a mentality of legalism, with all kinds of possibly awkward consequences, it also created an ecclesiology that saw the Church, as it were *suspended by a network of accountability,* from the ruling authority of the pope, appointing bishops and the bishops ordaining and licensing priests, rather than being *sacramentally created* by Jesus offering himself up to the Father and to us in his eucharistic body, making *us* into his Body, the Church, which then obviously had to organize itself, with some necessary rules and regulations and authorities, but not *deriving its very being and essence* from these as much as from the sacramental action of Christ, in the power of the Holy Spirit.

One implication of this late medieval view of the Church was that those, for whatever reason, disconnected from the pope's central jurisdiction, could not be seen as genuinely parts of the Church of Christ.

And so it is that the relatively recent rediscovery, or re-realization, of the fact that the being and life of the Church is really rooted in that sacramental action of Christ, has contributed to the understanding by both Orthodox and Catholics that, to quote the Agreed Statement of the Joint International Commission for Theological Dialogue between the Roman Catholic Church and the Orthodox Church,

> There exists then only one Church of God. The identity of one Eucharistic assembly with another comes from the fact that all with the same faith celebrate the same memorial, that all by eating the same bread and sharing the same cup become *the same unique body* of Christ into which they have been integrated by the same baptism . . . For this reason, the local church which celebrates the Eucharist, gathered around its bishop, is *not a section* of the body of Christ. [1]

1. Joint International Commission, *The Mystery of the Church,* 48–49.

It is not a *section*, a partial *fragment*, any more than one small eucharistic wafer is one *part* of the Body of Christ. Receiving a small host, we receive the *whole* Christ, the same whole Christ as the person next to us is receiving in another small host. Just as these two hosts are both the same *whole* Christ, in the same way each and every local church celebrating the same Eucharist is the same *whole* Body of Christ. And for this reason the early Fathers referred to the *local* church as *Catholic, whole, complete:* the word *catholic* meaning this *wholeness,* as much as it means universality.

And, while a whole theological movement in the Catholic Church through the last century has blossomed and developed a so-called *communion ecclesiology,* or, more pointedly, *eucharistic ecclesiology,* and prepared the perspectives of the Second Vatican Council, much credit has to go to the Orthodox theologian Nicholas Afanasiev, who was for this reason also invited to the Council, who broke ground early on by his book *L'Eglise du Saint-Esprit,* which of course also shifts the emphasis to the Holy Spirit as the *power-source* of this sacramental-eucharistic genesis of the Church, this sacramental-eucharistic ecclesiology, giving full ecclesial reality to every local church wherever the true Eucharist is celebrated.

But Afanasiev's eucharistic ecclesiology could be misconstrued in a sort of congregationalist sense, deducing from it a sacramental self-sufficiency of the local church, without reference to the other, identical, sister churches, making up and being identical with the universal church.

For the view that the Church is produced by the one and only valid and true Eucharist celebrated in every local church also means that the local church contains within itself the fullness of the *universal* catholic church. That is why the term *catholic church,* in the very earliest literature, was used in reference to the local church which was "catholic" in the sense that it was complete, as the just quoted document states, "not a section of the body of Christ," any more than one wafer is only a part of Christ's body. Each consecrated wafer, each Mass, and each local eucharistic assembly is *the whole* Christ, not a mere fragment, but, for that very reason, one and identical with every other local church being the whole Christ.

So, the implication of this fact is not that the local church is complete and self-sufficient, without any reference to all the other local churches, but precisely that, each local church is *sacramentally identical* with every other local church that celebrates the same one Eucharist, and thus *there is only one Church,* and that whole one Church is present in all the local churches that are identical and in communion with each other.

Now, without being able to go into the numerous further implications of this understanding of the Church in detail, let us just sketch an *overall portrait* of the Church understood as a thing born out of the celebration of the Eucharist.

We have already discussed how, already by *Baptism*, we are *grafted* into the Body of Christ, so the beginnings of the Church *predate,* so to speak, the celebration of the Eucharist. We have seen how the two key texts on Baptism give away the depth of this *immersion* that the average Christian, not understanding Greek and accustomed to our baby-sprinkling rites, doesn't even suspect.

The way Jesus described the whole process of what began by being immersed into his death and into his burial by immersion into water, is that, by that act we were actually immersed, through being joined to Christ, into the very *being of God the Holy Trinity:* in him we became sharers of their life: the new life that those eating his flesh and drinking his blood would never lose!

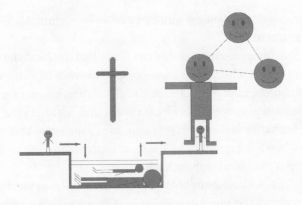

"=baptized (=plunged) into Christ Jesus we were baptized (=plunged) into his death; …
we went into the tomb with him and joined him in death, so that as Christ was raised from the
dead, … we too might live a new life." (Rom 6:3-4)

"Make disciples of all nations, baptizing (=plunging) them into (the name of)
the Father and of the Son and of the Holy Spirit." (Matt 28:19)

And so, this brings us to the deepest roots of eucharistic communion ecclesiology: the Communion, the Church that is created in this manner, is actually a participation of all of us in the life and being of the Holy Trinity. And so, this way of understanding the Church is not only eucharistic: it is *Trinitarian*. Last but not least, to return to the emphasis Afanasiev made in his presentation of eucharistic communion ecclesiology, the Church is seen this way as created by the *Holy Spirit* who, in the words of John Zizioulas, *constitutes* sacramentally what was historically *instituted* by Christ.

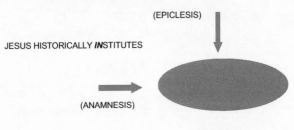

THE HOLY SPIRIT ESCHATOLOGICALLY *CON*STITUTES

(EPICLESIS)

JESUS HISTORICALLY *IN*STITUTES

(ANAMNESIS)

THE CHURCH

This pneumatological dimension of the Church's genesis complements and balances the christological dimension, as if to say Jesus *instituted* the Church *historically,* and the Holy Spirit *constituted* it *eschatologically,* as it were pulling it into its final and eternal future and identity, beyond its merely historical existence, and empowering it.

Of course, these two aspects of the Church being generated eucharistically are present in and can be read out of the eucharistic liturgy, as we have seen. The *Institution Account* of the words of Jesus represents the *historical institution;* and the *epiclesis,* our invocation of the Holy Spirit for the consecration of the bread and wine (consecratory epiclesis) and, through them, the consecration of the assembly into Church—the Body of Christ and the mystical communion with the Holy Trinity (communion epiclesis)—represents the *pneumatological completion* and fruition of the work of Christ.

In the last chapter we saw how this dynamic is articulated in the eucharistic liturgy. But now, to complete our exploration, let us at least sketch a portrait of the Church understood as a thing born out of the celebration of the Eucharist. Actually I suspect that that portrait is already emerging from what has been said so far.

There was a wonderful little book years ago, written by the late Cardinal Avery Dulles, entitled *Models of the Church.* In that book Dulles described—among others—a model he called the *institutional* model of the Church. That would be the model, the self-understanding of the Church that developed in the second millennium in the Western Church, as we saw earlier, as East and West drifted apart, and Roman juridicism, legalism, helped shape a notion of the Church as being a society historically founded, instituted by Jesus, for the purpose of carrying out its salvific mission and being equipped to do that with the authority and power of her Founder. *The Church making the Eucharist*—among other things.

We did point out how this was a one-sided emphasis, with a number of unfortunate side effects. You might say it resulted in an ecclesial culture which, to some extent, we still experience. A thousand years of collective habits and attitudes are not easy to modify.

Now, on the other hand, in this gradually recovered, retrieved, *eucharistically* based communion ecclesiology, we have a *restored balance* between an overwhelmingly historical and organizational emphasis, linked to the historical Jesus, and the sometimes almost neglected spiritual-mystical dimension of the Holy Spirit bringing-into-being a sacramental union with God in creating this wonderful Mystery of the Church. Those of you familiar with Dulles's "models" will find that a blend of his "mystical communion" model and his "sacramental" model corresponds best to our eucharistic communion model, brilliantly described both in the Second Vatican Council's *Lumen gentium,* in the chapter entitled "The Mystery of the Church," and in the Munich document of the Orthodox-Catholic joint Commission, quoted earlier.[2]

In a Church that we understand to be the fruit of the Eucharist, we learn how to "read" the characteristics of the Church and of the Christian out of the Mystery of the Eucharist, deepening what has happened to all of us in Baptism, where we have had to do some dying, in that death becoming one with each other in Christ, and moving together into his risen life, to be fully revealed in the eschaton, but already present, so that the emphasis in what we understand the Church to be will be on our *intimate share in the being and life* of the most Holy Trinity: Father, Son, and Holy Spirit.

Instead of seeing the Church as a multinational corporation, run on managerial expertise, political know-how, upward mobility, and juridical control, the Church is *the event of our sacramental-mystical communion with each other and with God in an eschatological intimacy already realized.*

That, dear reader, is the significance of rediscovering the Eucharist as the central act of *the Church realizing herself* as the covenantal Communion in Christ with the Triune God.

---

2. Joint International Commission, *The Mystery of the Church*, published in McPartlan, *One in 2000?*

CHAPTER 5

Luther on the Eucharist
and the Church

WE HAVE BEEN EXPLORING various aspects of our being drawn into
the Communion of the very Blessed Trinity, into that Communion
which is the very *being* of God, through our baptismal-eucharistic
insertion, making us into *the Church,* that extension and participation of that great divine Communion.

Understanding the nature of the Church in this way is a very
ancient understanding, which has been happily rediscovered,
retrieved, and reemphasized in our own time, by Orthodox and
Catholics, as well as by Anglicans and some Protestants, opening
new possibilities for them to rediscover each other as members
of the same Mystery, belonging to the same body, and designed,
by God's own plan, to be gathered together in the same divine
embrace.

While this recovery has accelerated and intensified in the
twentieth century, it had slow and timid beginnings for quite a
long time, in fact, was never quite lost. One interesting pioneer, a
Reformation voice, was Martin Luther himself. So, it is appropriate
for us to recognize this voice and take a brief look at his attempts to
formulate what we now take for granted, that "the Eucharist makes
the Church."

The full insight into what has come to be called *communion ecclesiology* is that the Church is our being gathered together in an *organic communion,* a body, that is not only the Body of Christ, with all the astounding implications of a mystical identification between us as church and the very Person of Jesus, but more, through that fact, as a very sharing in the life of the Trinitarian Communion of Father, Son, and Holy Spirit.

This view of the Church as the Trinitarian Communion into which we are literally *divinized* by our baptismal immersion is by no means new—as said above, it was a rediscovery, largely gained through our twentieth-century forebears who, more than anyone before, have thoroughly researched the beginnings of Christianity. The far-reaching implications of this recovered emphasis are only just beginning to be understood.

Martin Luther, as you will see, can be identified as an early forerunner of this rediscovery, in particular of the generative connection between the Eucharist as the generator of the Church and the Church itself. The bread becomes the Body that becomes the Church.

It must be said of course that, the Eucharist, the Lord's Supper, had always been celebrated on the Lord's Day, the day of his Resurrection, as the *only* new and distinctively Christian act of worship and act of *communion,* distinct from the Jewish Sabbath; otherwise the first Christians continued the Jewish practices and patterns of daily prayer. However, over the centuries there had been a very slow, subtle, and gradual shift of emphasis from the earliest stress on Jesus giving us his sacrificial Body and Blood so that we could become participants in it, becoming that Body by ingesting it, to an awe and fascination with the consecrated elements themselves, to the point where actual *communion* at each celebration became less frequent and normative. We might say that the attention had shifted from the actual *purpose* of the Eucharist *making the Church*, to the Church making and venerating the Eucharist.

It is at this point that I want to refer to an early work of Luther, addressing this distortion and trying to restore the proper perspective on the Eucharist, not stopping as it were with the bread becoming the Body, but pushing this fact to its finality by stressing that, through that sacramental transformation, it was the *Church* that became the Body of Christ, *that* being the point of the whole sacramental exercise.

The work I am referring to is entitled *The Blessed Sacrament of the Holy and True Body of Christ, and the Brotherhoods*. It dates from 1519 and expresses Luther's thought on the Eucharist *before* he became embroiled in the Reformation battles about the real presence, which, paradoxically, dragged him back to the same misfocusing which he so clearly sought to correct in this earlier work. The German Luther scholar Paul Althaus says:

> There can be no question that this development restricted and impoverished the doctrine of the sacrament of the Lord's Supper and the celebration of this meal in the Lutheran Church compared with its fullness among primitive Christians.[1]

Of course this was written forty years ago, and Lutheran thought and practice today is vastly different from what it was then, thanks to the liturgical and ecumenical movements.

What *was* the point of this early Lutheran corrective? To put it simply, that, "the *significance* (=what the sacrament signifies) and/ or *effect* of this sacrament is *the Communion of saints*."[2] Now "the Communion of saints," for Luther as for the early church, is the Church itself, both on earth and in heaven. So, he points out that the Latin term for partaking of the sacrament is to *communicate* or *commune*, and that, in this way, our eucharistic sharing means not only that Christ becomes food and drink for us, but that we also become food and drink for each other. To paraphrase this, our eucharistic communion builds us into an *organic communion* or *organism of life*—much the same thought St. Paul intended to express by describing the Church as the Body of Christ, in which we are members of one another, because we partake of the same

1. Althaus, *The Theology of Martin Luther,* 322.
2. Luther, *Luther's Works,* 35:50.

loaf. In other words, as St. Augustine expressed it, "the Eucharist *makes the Church."*

The benefit of this communion, in Luther's words, is "that all the spiritual possessions of Christ and his saints are shared with and become the common property of him who receives this sacrament."[3] But then, receiving the benefit of this communion is not the end-point either; in fact, it furnishes the foundation for all Christian conduct and action, as implied by this communion.

> When you have partaken of this sacrament [Luther continues] your heart must go out in love and learn that this is a sacrament of love. As love and support are given to you, you in turn must render love and support to Christ in his needy ones.[4]

In fact, Christian existence and Christian morality are explicitly seen as being Eucharistic and ecclesial, in other words implications of eucharistic communion, when Luther applies the eucharistic mandate of Christ to daily living.

> When Christ instituted the sacrament, he said, "This is my body which is given for you, this is my blood which is poured out for you. As often as you do this, remember me." It is as if he were saying, "I am the Head, I will be the first to give himself for you. I will make your suffering and misfortune my own and will bear it for you, so that you in turn may do the same for me and for one another, allowing all things to be common property, in me, and with me."[5]

I am not sure about Luther's thinking about the sacrificial dimension of the Eucharist at this early stage, but it may be suggested that a sense of it is implied between the lines when he speaks of Christ giving himself for us, so that we also should do the same for him and for one another.

---

3. Luther, *Luther's Works,* 35:51.
4. Ibid., 54.
5. Ibid., 54–55.

Then Luther goes on to urge the *frequent reception* of the sacrament to nurture our Christian eucharistic living, and criticizes the celebrations of the Eucharist without people receiving communion, a practice that had developed in the Middle Ages.

To sum up the early Luther's eucharistic ecclesiology, we can say that the point of the Eucharist is that, by means of a loaf of bread and a cup of wine transformed into the Body and Blood of our Lord, we, who receive them, become that loaf and that cup, transformed into Christ. If you like, as a result of communion, we are the sacramental bearers of the real presence of Christ to each other and to the world, and of course our task is to continue doing what Christ has done "for the life of the world."

Now, while this perspective already gives us a valuable insight into the eucharistic constitution of the Church, what Luther is remarkably thin on is the Trinitarian grounding and completion of this eucharistic communion ecclesiology. Of 464 pages on *The Theology of Martin Luther,* the earlier quoted Paul Althaus has *one page and a half on Luther's thoughts regarding the Trinity!* And what is stated there in so many words is simply that Luther *had accepted the doctrine* of the Trinity, because he considered it to be scriptural. Period. He was not alone in his lack of appreciation for the utterly foundational importance, not of the *doctrine* of the Trinity, as some sort of an intellectual abstraction of no practical importance, but of the very dynamic of God's *being as Trinitarian Communion,* the *relational pattern* of God's irreducible plurality in indivisible Communion, as the source and pattern of everything that exists. As the Methodist scholar Geoffrey Wainwright has pointed out, quoting the German Jesuit Karl Rahner, for most of our history the doctrine of the Trinity may well have been dropped from the books, and it would not have made much difference.[6] However, the twentieth century has seen a genuine ecumenical rediscovery of the Trinity, with a multitude of very important implications.

So, how does this rediscovery affect our eucharistic ecclesiology? In fact, *it grounds it.* For what would be the point of human

6. Reference unavailable.

communion in the Church; what would even be the point of communion with Jesus in the Body of Christ, if, with and in Christ, we were not brought into the divine communion of Father, Son, and Holy Spirit?!

On the Feast of the Presentation of the Lord we conclude the liturgical cycle that celebrates the joining of human and divine in the redemptive Communion of the Incarnation. It was that act of God whereby he extended the Communion of Father and Son and Holy Spirit to assume into it the humanity conceived in Mary's womb. And it is into that humanity, and by means of that humanity, that we are immersed by Baptism and embodied by the Eucharist into the Trinitarian Communion of the divine Persons themselves.

And so, we can say that the whole purpose and consummation of our eucharistic Communion in the Church is that, by means of our union with Christ, we may be taken into the "inner circle" of the divine life, the divine family. It is this ultimate goal of our divinization in that Communion that the whole history of salvation, redemption, recapitulation moves toward. And the Eucharist is the central means whereby this becomes a reality.

And so, in the famous fifteenth-century icon imaging the Three Persons of the Holy Trinity, we see them as it were seated around the eucharistic table, sharing in the sacrificial banquet that celebrates and realizes every level of communion, from the divine circle of Three, providing the eternal model for all that exists—in plurality and unity—to the ecclesial circle, making explicit the shape of the world, the cosmos, this organically relational universe, in which life is a symphony of diversity in communion.

CHAPTER 6

Obedience and Love

Marriage, Monastery, Trinity

(Ephesians on Marriage – Obedience to the Abbot –
The Fatherhood of the Father)

A COMMON SOURCE OF embarrassment for modern Westerners today is the text in Ephesians 5:21–33 that once was a standard reading for marriage services, calling for the wife to obey her husband
and submit to him in all things. The text has been thoughtlessly
abused by husbands taking their right to oppress and control their
wives for granted, demanding submission to them in all things,
while considering themselves free agents, above all such accountability, not owing any explanation for their actions and choices,
even to the extent of making major purchases without consulting
the person with whom they share their common family resources.
The pattern is often loudly proclaimed as a typical Middle Eastern
abuse of women, who could be stoned to death for adultery, while
the men are not subject to such severe censure. Yet, in somewhat
subtler forms this view of the wives' responsibility is widespread
in our own society, often with more or less explicit recourse to the
above-mentioned biblical text.

For anyone familiar with the ideal of St. Benedict, who in some ways modeled his monastic community on the family, the parallel to monastic obedience immediately suggests itself, and it is only a short step from there to the pattern of relationships within the Blessed Trinity, the "headship" of husband and abbot being compared to the role of God the Father, or of Christ, the head of the Church. For the Trinitarian pattern has modeled the order of the universe as a web of relationships, created and held together by the Communion of Father, Son, and Holy Spirit, grounding the Church in its fundamental nature, and sacramentalizing that communion in Marriage.

However, the critical text needs to be understood in the cultural context in which it has its origins, and it is obvious that it has been interpreted with various emphases, according to the changing times, places, and mentalities.

The obedience demanded of monks to their abbot can and has also been interpreted in differing styles and on occasion abused in the same way a wife's submission to her husband has been. It can be—and has been—construed as a mindless mortification of the self before an arbitrary, superior, and autocratic authority, "just because," *submission* to the will of another—a *superior*—being of the essence. (Curiously, such "obedience" is often set in opposition to following one's own conscience, as if the decision to obey were not the work of an informed conscience.)

However, on reading the *Rule of St. Benedict,* it quickly becomes obvious that the fatherhood of the abbot is modeled more on the primacy of God the loving Father within his Trinity of equals, rather than on that of a military commander. The abbot "should always remember what he is called (*Abba*=Father)."[1]

Interestingly, the image then immediately shifts to Christ, whose representative the abbot is said to be, but the Trinitarian background, even if not explicitly acknowledged, cannot be missed.

---

1. St. Benedict, *Rule,* chapter 2.

The abbot is normatively elected by the monks from among their number, so he is not an outside superior imposed on a group of inferiors, but a member—now the father—of the coenobitic family. And while obedience to the abbot, within the terms of the same *Rule* that the abbot himself is required to obey together with his monks, is a fundamental principle of monastic life, the reason for this is given as the Abbot standing in the place of Christ (or the Father). Hence we are referred to the Trinitarian pattern, in which the Son obeys the Father ("I have come . . . not to do my own will but . . . the will of the one who sent me"[2]), remembering that, despite the primacy of the Father, there is a fundamental equality among the Three Persons of the Trinity. The will of the Eternal Son is by definition identical to that of the Father, and the destiny of Jesus is fulfilled by his human will agreeing with his divine will, which is one with his Father's!

As well, the fundamental structure of monastic obedience is all-pervasive, not restricted to obedience to the abbot, but designed for all in the community having a common mind and a communion of love. "Be united in your convictions and united in your love, with a common purpose and a common mind" (Phil 2:2). The monks must "obey" *each other* and anticipate each other's wishes. "The service of obedience is to be shown to all, not just the abbot, for by this road of obedience they shall travel to find God."[3] In fact, our very text on Marriage begins with "Give way *to one another* in obedience to Christ" (Eph 5:21). And so it becomes clear that "obedience," which is, as suggested by its etymology, a function of complete attention and effective hearing (*ob-audire*) of each other, is a harmonizing of the will with another out of love. In and of itself this effort is not a destruction of one's will before another and superior being, nor is it necessarily (or even ideally) unilateral.

It bears mentioning that the Ephesians text in question does originate, as does the whole of the Bible, in the same Middle

---

2. John 6:38, quoted by St. Benedict in *The Rule,* chapter 5 on obedience.

3. St. Benedict, *The Rule,* chapter 71.

Eastern region and culture where burqas are worn, women are forbidden to be seen in public without a male escort, study to obtain professional degrees, or drive a car. While some of these extremes are associated with extremist forms of Islam, the overwhelming success of that religion in the Middle East is not un-related to long-standing cultural/religious traditions and attitudes among the Semitic peoples in those regions, witnessed to even in the New Testament reports of the stoning of women caught in adultery, without a suggestion that the men implicated would also be subject to such punishment. And so, what the text intends to teach about obedience, an effort to bring one's will and choices into harmony with those of another out of love, is *imaged* in a vertical, subordinationary structure between a superior and inferior, as it was commonly understood in that culture. Absolute authority and power of a superior over an inferior, rather than a communion of wills in love!

Within that culture (in which neither usury nor slavery were questioned) it was an accepted fact that the husband was the "head" of the family. And it was within that structure that the family relationship was likened to the "marriage" of Christ with his Church, the absolute mutual love being expressed by Jesus loving his "bride" to the point of *giving his life* for her, and the "bride" loving her husband by conforming her will to his in a communion of love. (The all-pervasive gift of one's life is surely not a lesser gift than conforming one's will to that of another!) Clearly, both converging and mutual gestures can be seen in sacrificial terms, much as the ritual sealing the Covenant of union between God and his people at Sinai was a sacrificial communion meal (Exod 24).

As this culturally well understood image of Marriage is explicitly referred to the union of the Church with Christ, the Trinitarian/ecclesiological context makes it obvious that we are taught a lesson about a Communion grounded in and modeled on the Trinity, where the unity of wills is a function of that Communion of love which is the fundamental nature of God, of Christ, and of the Church, sacramentalized in Marriage.

There is of course an inevitable subordination of creature to Creator, and hence the Christ-Church relationship being a sacramental image of marriage can be (mis-)read as absolute submission, if the difference between the two realities, and the cultural context, are ignored. The relationship of love and communion is the same in both cases, but Christ is the divine head of the human church—even as it is divinized by him—while husband and wife are equal human partners, who, by harmonizing their wills in a communion of love, live out and sacramentalize the love and union of Christ with his Church.

It is then important to understand that the Ephesians text is urging an equally unselfish giving of self on the part of the husband as it is requiring of the wife, in a sacramental communion imaging and realizing for them the communion that exists between Christ and his Church and, indeed, between the Father and the Son and the Holy Spirit. And it is in this total gift of self in a communion of love that their destiny in God's design is fulfilled.

CHAPTER 7

The Great Commandment
of Communion

THE REALIZATION OF OUR utter unworthiness before God, on the one hand, and the unimaginable holiness of God, to which we are called nonetheless, on the other hand, must be followed by the understanding that this unbridgeable gap has actually been bridged by God's gift of himself to us. God has initiated a relationship, by entering into a Covenant with us, by actually forging a unity, a communion, between his divine being and nature, his unique holiness and utter otherness on the one hand, and our own humanity on the other hand. God has united these two in the single Person of his Son, his Personal Image and Word, in and through which/whom we had been created for God, so that, through this divine man and human God, we should be drawn into his very own Trinitarian Communion.

While this can only be God's own doing, that we are factually transformed and divinized, something we could not achieve by our own efforts, we are nevertheless enabled, and then challenged, by this gift, to put into practice, to operationalize, what we have become—this being our moral/spiritual assignment, as Christians.

When you think about it, this reflection really amounts to a more accurate understanding of the challenge of Christian morality, as not so much being conformity to a *moral code*, "fulfillment"

of a set of *commandments*, as it is attending to, cherishing, cultivat-
ing, and growing in a *personal relationship*. This is a relationship
with another Person, indeed, a community or communion of a
unity-in-the-plurality of other Persons, both divine and human.
It is this that is basically summed up in the Great Commandment,
"to love the Lord our God with all our heart and with all our soul
and with all our mind and with all our strength, and our neighbor
as ourselves." And the horizon, the goal of this commandment, is
infinite.

Now it is crucially important to understand this *love language*
in terms of *ontology*, if we are going to understand it rightly in
terms of morality. Love is not required of us, or even desired by us,
simply because it is a nice addition or enrichment to our existence,
or a good that improves our life. Love is the behavioral name for
the cohesion, the relationality, the communion that accounts for
our very *being*.

In other words, love is not a good thing, an extra that is added
to being—as if beings had to first exist, and then they could choose
to love. Love is the *condition*, the *presupposition* of our very being
and life. That is why it is the First and Great Commandment, and
that is why everything, all the law and the prophets, are summed
up in it, and every behavioral requirement is a particular implication and application of that fundamental *condition of being* which,
if we go against it, results in permanent death.

But that of course means that the measure of living up to
that law is the *cultivation of our relationship, the care for our communion*, as care for our very being. The moral good is whatever
contributes positively to that relationship, that communion, what
cultivates it, nurtures it. And the moral evil is whatever damages it.
In fact, if we remember that persons are "*subsistent relationships,*"
then the measure of our morality will be seen in the quality of our
interactions with the other person, be it God or a human, or any
part of creation, because that communion is what gives us *being*.

This unique and personal relationship furthermore means
that the material *content* of our relationship, the issues and

concerns, the challenges and difficulties, are not exactly the same as those of somebody else's relationship with God, or with others. The vocation, the call, the expectations are to some extent as unique as the relationships.

To simply take a general and impersonal list of do's and don'ts and examine myself against such a list is therefore not quite fine-tuned enough for *this* relationship of *mine*.

If you think of it, were the issue simply that we all had to conform to the same objective and universal code of behavior, we could have a chart on the wall and record our performance there and compare ourselves to each other, being able to judge our own and each other's performance.

One of the reasons why we must not, and cannot, judge each other, or indeed ourselves in such a comparative fashion, is because we do not have the comparative data, the givens of each relationship. So, this is not the best way of tending and tracking our own personal relationship with God, or with each other.

Furthermore, not only do we need to shift from impersonal moral code to *personal relationship* as our guide, we also should shift from the idea—suggested by the moral code approach—that we can *fulfill* the commandments and be done with them, as it were, to a very different challenge, and that is that the Great Commandment, on which "hang all the law and the prophets," is really unfulfillable, because it is not a finite and quantifiable task, a list of items we can tick off, but an infinite horizon of divine being and love, towards which we must strive, in which we must progress, but which will only be fulfilled in the parousia, and *then* by God. As my German Professor of Moral Theology in Rome put it, the Christian moral challenge is a *Zielgebot* rather than an *Erfuellungs-gebot*—a *goal* or *target*-commandment, rather than a benchmark that we can reach and then relax and say: "What now, Lord, I have fulfilled all the Commandments?!" as the rich young man in the Gospel put it.

So, in this way of looking at our challenge, it makes more sense that we can *aim* at perfection in our relationship with and participation in God's holiness and love, because these are infinite and unquantifiable goals or horizons that draw us on, irrespective of where we may be along the way, and we can never say we have fulfilled them, or we have gone half of the way, or we are total failures.

The reason St. John can say we are all sinners is because no matter where we are, how far we have progressed on the road, we always fall short of the infinite. That is also why when someone like St. Teresa of Avila said she was such a great sinner, she wasn't kidding or being phony. She knew she still fell infinitely short of the goal: God.

This is another reason why it is not possible to compare ourselves to each other, as if to say, John has fulfilled the commandments and Bill has not, Pat is closer to perfection than Gil. It is not a *race* where we compete against each other, or measure ourselves against a chart. Instead, it is our own natural and supernatural gifts and weaknesses that contextualize our progress on this infinite journey, and the measure of our running towards our final fulfillment is the secret of every individual path, the gains and the bumblings of our own unique love affair with God, in the midst of our own specific challenges.

And in a sense the same principle applies to all of our relationships, all of our successes and failures in loving each other. Which is the reason why we are in no position to judge one another: because we haven't got the data.

I recently had a conversation with a teacher who expressed her dissatisfaction with the grading system, saying it was only helpful to the middle range of students, who would be stimulated to improve their grades. The top students had to make no effort to get an "A" and could therefore slack off and not do their best, and the weak students were discouraged to the point of giving up. It struck me that this was the very same issue we are talking about in terms of our life with God, our particular moral challenges to love wholeheartedly. It would almost seem more helpful to have our own tunnel to pass through, without being able to look sideways and compare our progress, either to others or to a scale or chart.

We have the natural tendency to say, "I wish I could be like Joe or Mary," and, especially in our youth, we want to model ourselves on somebody we admire. But, in the end, I am not called to be Moses or Elijah, Peter, Paul, or St. Benedict, or St. Teresa, or Fr. George, but me. And God has a very special idea about the unique kind of a guy he wants me to become, or, the unique *relationship* he wants to have with me, the unique *web* of relationships he has fashioned me for, or, to put it even more accurately, the kind of *guy the unique web of relationships he made me part of should shape me into.*

And that goes for each and every one of us. And our uniqueness is the function of *the unique relationship* of love that exists between him and each of us and which in fact creates us to be who we are. He loved us and thought us up before we ever existed, and that is how he *loved us—willed us—into being.* And our uniqueness is also determined by the unique place we occupy in the web of relationships within which we are created and called to be who we are meant to be.

When you come to think of it, the idea of my "fulfilling" God's expectations of me today is rather strange, unless I have a finite, quantitative job description laying down precisely *how much* I must love God and my neighbor. How much and not more. The Great Commandment actually tells us: "with all [our] heart, and with all [our] soul, and with all [our] mind, and with all [our] strength." And our neighbor as ourselves. And that's what is meant by a *Zielgebot*—a commandment without limit.

And this really brings up the connection between holiness and "unconditional love." For if we truly understand that holiness is defined as the totally unique *otherness* of God, unapproachable and inaccessible to creatures, and we are called to participate in that (uncreated) holiness, and if it is true that therefore holiness is not some quantitative moral improvement, then the question is, in what way can this uncreated divine quality be realized, operationalized, translated into some kind of human quality. What does it consist in, if it is not simply self-improvement?

The only key to finding an answer to this question is Jesus, because the whole point of the Incarnation has been to translate what is specifically divine into what is human. So, just as we say that in the face of Jesus we see the face of God, it is *the kind of humanity* that Jesus embodied that gives us an indication of the nature of divinity. And if the totally transparent and unrestrained, un-withholding, unconditional, and unqualified self-giving and Communion between Father, Son, and Holy Spirit is indeed God's being ("as Communion"), then it is in *that* precisely that the uniqueness of the divine nature consists, and that is what we call love—unconditional love which, in the case of God, is the most fundamental ontological given. "God *is* love." Perfect love. *Agape.*

Well, then, apparently, it is this that we have understood through Jesus, it is this essence of divinity that was transposed into human reality by Jesus, and it is this that models for us the unreserved and complete form of love spelled out in the Great Commandment.

Now there is occasionally some debate about "unconditional love," supposedly best approximated by a mother's love for her most undeserving children, and our idealists would tell us that we all should love unconditionally. I personally have always maintained that *agape*, that totally outgoing and unconditional love, is something only God is capable of, and that totally unconditional love is impossible for humans. It is only realism to recognize that we need love *input*, if we are going to be capable of love *output*. And so this brings us back to the old doctrine of grace: what is impossible for us by human nature is given to us by grace, sanctifying grace, the gift of participating in the nature and virtues and love of God himself.

And it also means that the love we are commanded to practice, unconditionally, with our whole heart and mind and soul and strength, is not a matter of feelings, but one of the will: a decision to act in faith, and to *want* the good of the other.

There is a lovely expression in Italian for "I love you": "*Ti vo-glio bene*" = I want your good, I want you well, I want what is good for you. I may not *like* you, your way of being and acting may make me dislike you, unable to enjoy you, since you don't make me *feel good*, but I want your good, nothing but the best for you. *Ti voglio bene*. And so, what Charlie Brown said to Lucy is quite possible: "Of course I love mankind. It's *people* I can't stand." But that still means I have to *act out that love*, even if my will has to overpower my natural dislikes.

Now there is an important difference between objective behavior, outward norms of acceptable and desirable conduct, social intercourse, on the one hand, and the personal, internal efforts, gifts and challenges, within which we work towards our forever unfinished goal spelled out in the Great Commandment, on the other hand.

In *Canon Law* there is a useful distinction made between the external forum and the internal forum, and this distinction has very practical implications. The external forum deals with the visible behaviors that have obvious public, societal dimensions and effects on others. But the internal forum is strictly between the individual and God, and the measure is our love and intentions and understanding, not the measurable impact our actions or failures have had on others.

This distinction then is important for ourselves, as we may well fall short of the ideal behavior in our own life, or the goals we have set for ourselves, while in fact exerting our will to love. Then the measure for our conscience is simply how much we have loved or failed to love God and our brothers and sisters, not the actual deeds or omissions, the measurable outcomes of our efforts. We are measuring ourselves against the *Zielgebot* of striving to approach the infinite challenge of God's love, God's holiness.

This distinction is also immensely important pastorally. In fact, we see a lot of church debate that totally ignores this distinction and tries to change the moral code to suit the particular orientation or difficulty of certain individuals, and then loudly condemns those "rigorists" who have no consideration for the weaknesses or inclinations of others.

The pastorally correct answer of course is that we do have those codes to spell out some practical norms, the shape of normative behavior. But it is whatever is morally possible for each particular person within the context of their personal relationship with God, and within God's infinite *Zielgebot* of perfect love, that God is asking of us. And this must be worked out in each conscience.

We talked about a twofold shift in looking at our morality and spirituality. Using the Commandments as an objective, external yardstick is certainly useful as a benchmark of correct, normative behavior. But doing *only* that has two shortcomings. One is that it can give us the smug illusion that we have essentially fulfilled the commandments, that "I'm OK, Jack," "I am better than that publican," and it is perfectly all right for me to coast along and not be concerned about the tremendous task: to be holy, as God is holy. And, on the other hand, we can despair and lose hope, even to the point of giving up, if we consistently fall short of the objective benchmark of some commandment, or some other external expectation.

Another shortcoming of just looking at the moral code is that it is an *impersonal* attempt to conform to some *external* norms, rather than understanding the essence of God's call as being love: to love him with all that we have and all that we are, and to love each other as ourselves. The Great Commandment *transcends* the moral code: it is a challenge to love and to communion, which cannot simply be objectified.

To sum up, Christian perfection or holiness is not about checking ourselves against ten commandments as if against an objective code of behavior, and measuring our performance, even comparing ourselves to others on that score. The Summary of the Law that Christ has given us is the Law of Love, in other words the call and challenge to love with all that we have and with all that we do and with all that we are. It is this *all* that is the measure. Whatever we've got is the measure.

This is the mystery of an interpersonal relationship, a communion of love that actually has created us and keeps on creating us. It is as unique to us as our personal identity is. And, furthermore, its horizon, its perspective, its goal is infinite. It can no more be fulfilled and completed in any finite sense in this life than the ocean can be filled and completed by one or two little rivers trickling into it.

I love the vision of this life-task articulated by the Benedictine vow of *conversio morum*: a lifelong commitment to *continuous conversion,* a lifelong attentiveness to our relationship, and seeing, evaluating, choosing all things in the light of that relationship.

So, we are dealing with a love affair—or more properly I should say a marriage of infinite perspectives. And we have to give ourselves to its pursuit with all our imagination, every desire, and the knowledge that nothing, but nothing can fulfill better who we are than our complete giving of ourselves to it—to God, to them, to all. And the only possible measure is to see if we have been as wholehearted as we could be in this. St. Paul tells us:

> It does not make the slightest difference to me whether you, or indeed any human tribunal, find me worthy or not. I will not even pass judgment on myself. True, my conscience does not reproach me at all, but that does not prove that I am acquitted: the Lord alone is my judge. There must be no passing of premature judgment. Leave that until the Lord comes: he will light up all that is hidden in the dark and reveal the secret intentions of men's hearts. Then will be the time for each one to have whatever praise he deserves from God. (1 Cor 4:3–5)

And just remember the praise the poor widow received from Jesus, even though what she'd put into the collection was only a mite. Some days we can do no better than that. And the only measure is our wholeheartedness.

CHAPTER 8

Communion, Reconciliation, Public and Private Sins

A TROUBLING DILEMMA SOMETIMES presents itself to the practicing Catholic: "Can I go to communion today, or must I go to Confession first?" Another way of phrasing the question is: "Am I in the state of grace or not? For, if I am not, I will be committing sacrilege by going to communion, thereby adding one more serious sin to what I am already guilty of." And yet another related question is: "Is what I have done a serious, 'mortal' sin or not? Do I need to go to Confession or not?"

These questions are the products of centuries of development in interpreting what communion, *being* in communion or being in effect excommunicated means, what the nature and proper use of sacramental Reconciliation is, and how we distinguish between sins that result in effectively excluding us from communion and therefore require us to be sacramentally reconciled and those that are not as serious as that.

A look at the early practice of the Church in this regard and the development in the use of the Sacrament of Reconciliation may be helpful in resolving the practical conundrum of when confession is absolutely necessary before going to communion.

A very important realization emerging from the study of sacramental liturgy, its history and theology, is that sacraments—and liturgy in general—are *public* rites of the Church as community, not purely private, individual devotional exercises. They are acts of the community; they have a community-related function, and are therefore the business of the Community.

The very name of holy *Communion* indicates that it is a sacrament of *communion*, of belonging to the Body (of Christ, which is the Church) by sharing in the sacramental Body of Christ. And *excommunication*, whether by a public canonical act of the Church or by an act by which a person automatically cuts himself off from the community, logically bars that person from the *sacrament* (sign) of communion. It is also important to note the *relational* nature, both of belonging to the communion and of damaging and being severed from that communion.

Now, in the early church, a person who was severed from the Communion/community of the Church and therefore from full participation in the Eucharist, and wished to reverse the process and heal the separation, was required to be restored to communion by sacramental Reconciliation, a public rite, as well as by doing some penance, both of which were publicly observable acts, restoring the person to the community. And the acts that severed a person from the community were *public* sins, that is acts that obviously had a public dimension, damaging the community. In the early church these were understood to be of three kinds: apostasy (or the public rejection of the faith), murder, and adultery.

It is important to note that these sins required *public* Reconciliation, because they were *public* sins, visibly damaging the Community in their relationships.

It was over some 600 years of development that this *public* interpretation of both sins and reconciliation gradually shifted to an emphasis on the individual, private conscience and "mortal" versus "venial" sins, without reference to the community. And so, the sacrament of Reconciliation became ever more a private, individual *sacrament of Penance*, hidden from the public eye, and becoming a means to clear the conscience by obtaining God's forgiveness for even private sins.

Now, the forgiveness of God for private sins can be sought in private prayer. The requirement of *sacramental* reconciliation was originally only for the three kinds of *public* sins cutting a person off from the community. This requirement was then, in the course of the above-described development, transferred to "mortal" sins, even when they had no public implications.

In the process of this development, of course, moral and pastoral treatises discussed the nature of sins more and more independently of their public dimension, and stressing the inward and individual conscience's role in freely, knowingly, and willingly offending God (not the community and relationships within it). And so, the need to make use of the sacrament of Reconciliation or Penance became related to the seriousness of the sin, even if it was entirely a hidden and private act—or even thought. And, even so, there are circumstances in which a private act of penance and prayer for forgiveness, with the intention of subsequently confessing the sin in question, is considered sufficient preparation for communion.

It may be helpful to understand this development, when thinking about the nature of and need for the sacrament of Reconciliation/Penance, in relationship to entirely private sins that have no public/community dimension.

Apostasy can obviously be a very public act of leaving the Church or/and espousing a cause, sect, or movement that is incompatible with the Catholic faith and membership in the Church. A private and personal conviction that is in conflict with the teachings of the Church is not a public act of apostasy that would excommunicate a person.

Murder is a rather straightforward case of a very public act, which can scarcely ever be considered a "private" sin.

Adultery, that is the breaking up of a marriage, is equally public and cannot be hidden. An extramarital act of a sexual nature that has not been obviously destructive to the marriage, however, as privately sinful as it may be, is not necessarily a public offense. The question is, therefore, may such an offense be a matter for

63

private reconciliation before God, without absolutely requiring sacramental Confession?

The suggestion of this inquiry is not to diminish or reevaluate the *seriousness* of certain offences, but simply to suggest that the Church's practice with regard to requiring sacramental Confession has not always been the same, and the overall history of this practice may suggest that our current expectation that sacramental absolution is always absolutely required for certain acts is not as obvious as we have been accustomed to believe. The sacraments, as liturgical acts, are, by definition, public and communal in nature, and Reconciliation originally was a public act to remedy public offences damaging the community. Its extended use for all sins is certainly a most valuable spiritual remedy, but may not be absolutely necessary in all cases of serious but private sins.

CHAPTER 9

Confession—the Sacrament of Spiritual Friendship

IN HIS BOOK ON the priesthood, *Diener der Freude (A Celebration of Priestly Ministry)*,[1] Cardinal Kasper recalls the deep and formative impact that hearing confessions had on his early years in the priesthood. He says that no other aspect of his ministry gave him such valuable pastoral experience as he had during the many hours he would spend in the confessional. These intimate conversations changed his style of preaching and transformed him, and made him understand the infinite mercy of God.

Reading that, the point was driven home to me how deprived we all are today of a genuine, shared journey of exploring the mercy, the call, the peculiar personal presence of God in each and every one of our lives. Sacramental Confession, so rare in our day, is a unique and privileged place where we can safely and openly share and explore the many aspects and quests of our spiritual lives.

The origins of this sacrament had to do with serious breaches of communion with the Church, and so, of necessity, frequent Confession was not the practice, but, over the centuries, it became refined and sophisticated into an encounter of exploration and counsel—a joint, shared quest for learning how better to

---

1. Kasper, *A Celebration of Priestly Ministry.*

implement God's designs in our lives, how to avoid the pitfalls and become more adept at navigating through life's conundra in the context of the love of God. How often can we freely engage in such a conversation, in the context of love and prayer, these days?

And so, it may be useful to see this precious gift as not only a rite to formally forgive sins, but as a veritable sacrament of spiritual friendship. What Cardinal Kasper remembers of the wonderful resource this sacrament was for his own formation and growth as a priest, deeply resonates with me. This sacrament is not only good for the "penitent," for the one who comes to the priest, in a more or less formal setting, to confess, to explore, to inquire, to share and converse. That overture is really a response to the priest's preaching and teaching as much as it is a reflection on the "penitent's" life opened up in confidence and trust.

Kasper says these encounters first and foremost affected his preaching—and changed him as a person, a priest, in his own life. How often does a priest feel—if he really puts himself into his preaching—that he is making a confession himself every time, hanging out his own struggle with God for all to look at, share, and learn from? And much of the time it feels as if he shouts into the void, and there is no reply, there is no turning it over, considering it, responding to it. Yet, sometimes his sermon is a lonely cry for spiritual friendship, for help: for it is through each other, that together we can grow and deepen.

The confessional is a private, safe, confidential place, where we can share questions, explorations, reactions we have to the Word of God and his call to us, and, yes, of course it is an incredible privilege for the priest to be trusted, to be able to be, at the very least, a sounding board, and, perhaps more often someone who is himself prodded to move on and deepen, but also who can share and apply the wisdom of the Church and his own experience to the life of another.

CHAPTER 10

The Church and Beyond in the Perspective of Trinitarian Communion

I WOULD LIKE TO begin by elaborating a bit on the title of this chapter, as it were, considering the *status quaestionis*.

The business of ecclesiology is not simply navel-gazing, in other words Christians thinking about who they are and how they are constituted as *Church*. Our interest must surely include how Christians are to be looking at the broader world beyond their ecclesial confines, how they may be *relating* to that broader world, whether we think about it simply as the wider human community, or even beyond that, as the entire cosmos—the environment in which that human community is placed, of which it is in fact an integral part and participant. It is a question of how we view and *relate* to that greater whole, of which we are part.

However, in order to think intelligently about any *relationship*, we do need to consider *who* it is that is doing the relating, and so, a certain amount of ecclesiology is inevitably part of this business; hence: "*The Church* and Beyond . . ." Of course the very *Trinitarian* perspective in which we want to do this exploration suggests that the *relating* itself is as primary as our identity, because it is the *nature of this relating itself* that in fact spells out who we are! And it is partly this particular twist, this new *emphasis on relating* that may be the most relevant insight of Trinitarian theology, perhaps a real breakthrough, with respect to both the Church and to what lies beyond. In other words, we can neither talk about *how we relate to the world* without doing some *ecclesiology*, nor can we have a proper understanding of the *Church* without considering this *relationship to the world which is constitutive* of the Church.

So, what about the matter of this *relational perspective*? On the face of it, it seems obvious that, whatever we consider, we do it from some sort of a perspective, an angle, a viewpoint, which will inevitably color our interpretation of reality. Our perspective is determined primarily by where we are located, and, related to that, by *who we are, how we think, what our equipment*—such as our spectacles—is like. And so, we say we want to look at this church-and-world problematics "from the perspective of *Trinitarian Communion*."

This particular perspective raises a further complication that I would just like to raise, without attempting to resolve it. As a theologian and an ecclesiologist, within the context of my discipline, I should find no difficulty in spending twenty minutes talking about the Three-Personal God, the *relationships* within the Three-in-One, the nature of their *Communion* and their operations *ad extra*: creating, redeeming, sanctifying, recapitulating. I should have even less difficulty talking another twenty minutes about the nature of the Church, as it is shaped to reflect this Trinitarian *Communion* character of God who, by means of this medium of the Church, means to incorporate human beings into the Trinity's own *Communion*. And then, a further twenty minutes could be an easy description of how this ecclesial Communion, fashioned after the character and nature of the originating Trinity itself, is the model, the making explicit, of the human community and of a beautifully interrelated, harmonious cosmos, as God had intended them to be.

The problem is that, doing this as a theologian, one is already presupposing an entire framework, taking it for granted that we have some sort of revealed information about this Trinity, from which we can and have deduced substantial insight, indeed, a perspective. We are looking at the Church as a reality, and the world, as a reality, and the relationship of the two, from the (presumed) perspective of the Trinity, from God's perspective, modeled on God's own self-constitution! The only niggling difficulty I would like to suggest is one that occurs to most of us as soon as someone, say our daughter, or son, or grandchild, or a parishioner, asks for an accounting for our belief, for a legitimation of this whole theological method of deriving supposed knowledge from supposed revelation. What do we know about the Trinity, and *how* do we know what we think we know?

Well, this is not going to be an essay in hermeneutics, but the very subject of Trinity-Church-world, and the suggestion that there is a common or corresponding structure, raises the inevitable question of *which way* we argue. Do we have an *ontological blueprint*, or do we *surmise from our experience*? In other words: do we know exactly how the Trinity is put together, so we can draw inferences for Church and world, or have we as human beings, over the millennia, experienced ourselves in a particular way, experienced the reality of the Church and of a people that has consciously and explicitly come to understand itself as having been fashioned through a Covenant with God, and then began to surmise what sort of a God it must be who has dealt with us thus?

Bringing the question to bear directly on our topic, I would like to submit that perhaps it goes both ways. For, as Scripture scholars suggest, some of the constructions of Scripture are backfilled from the experience of the Church, or of the Israelites, so that the experience actually *preceded* the story or the theological insight that we have been handed down as revelation. This is specifically stated about the creation narratives composed *after* the Covenant accounts, as well as of some New Testament accounts, for instance, of the form of Baptism, or of the Eucharist. So, it took some centuries of ecclesial experience to understand, and, indeed, to nail down the sacred writings that corresponded to that experience and understanding, and were hence deemed "canonical." As for the Trinity, it is only with hindsight from the Patristic period and the first few ecumenical councils that we can piece together the picture that had emerged only gradually.

But once the insights are had, they are shamelessly regarded as divinely inspired and revealed information regarding the ontological Reality of God, which then becomes the normative model for created reality, because this people consistently perceives itself to be divinely guided. If anyone objects that the information had been backfilled from experience, rather than handed down, all we can say is that the overwhelming experience of a people, a community, over millennia, has given ample foundation for a faith, a belief, a credible conviction that the information is accurate, and legitimate. And so, for the theologian, it becomes legitimate method to say: since we know such and such to be the case about God, we can predicate the following about the intended shapes and outcomes in the world.

Structurally, as I suggested before, my exposé would have to show the parallelism or correspondence between three layers of reality, if you like, three circles or discs, over each other. The Trinitarian God—a circle of Father, Son and Holy Spirit, perhaps remembered as depicted in the famous fifteenth-century icon of Andrei Rublyov (1); the Communion of the Church, where many are one—"members of one another" (2); and finally the world: the family of humanity in the first place, but as organic members of the great cosmic communion of "Gaia," if you want to personify this complexity of organic relationships (3).

In some ways Christians are very slow to read the message, both from below and from above. We are a divided and cantankerously divisive lot, *that* being our single most fundamental and most scandalous crime, perhaps the very root of all sin—against faith, against hope, and against love—often literally manifesting itself in criminal behavior against each other's lives, and against the life of the planet we live on. And so, the theologian's and ecclesiologist's claim that the Church in some way is the *sacramentum mundi*, sacramentally making explicit the shape of reality as intended by God, does admittedly beg the question. To say that the shape of reality as intended by and grounded in the Three-Personal God, from above, and, indeed, as discovered by scientists, from below, from the sub-atomic particles to the galaxies, and from the most primitive living organisms to the nature of human society and culture, is to be experienced in and through the Church, does indeed beg the question! And yet, if you will, the real paradox between *behavior* and the claimed and theologically interpreted *experience* of a people shaped by a Covenant into a *Communion*, reflecting and integrating with this otherwise unimaginable divine Reality of the ultimate being of One-in-Three, is perhaps an all the *more* convincing foundation for faith, because it stands *in spite of* the obvious shortcomings in behavior. *Credo quia absurdum!*

The point of this hermeneutical *excursus* has been simply that there is a *correspondence*, a common, reflected pattern between three layers of reality, the divine Communion, the Communion character of the Church, and the organic relationality of the world —humanity and cosmos. And, secondly, that we do not argue in one direction, either from the top down or from empirical evidence up, but from the very *correspondence* itself, which, instead of providing apodictic proof, simply offers credibility, grounds the faith, and thereby legitimatizes the theological discourse.

Having hopefully justified the approach I am taking, let me sketch the pattern of this correspondence in a bit more detail. The three layers or three circles reflect the same structure. The normative and formative first layer or circle is the being and life of a God who is a Communion of a plurality-in-one. For this remarkable ultimate being, as the Greek theologian Metropolitan John Zizioulas has put it, *being is communion.*[1] This essentially means that it is impossible to distinguish between, or separate, God's *being* or *existence* from the *relationships* or *relationality* or active *relating* that is the life or activity of God. This is basically a new way of saying the same thing as *God is love*, meaning that *God is the action of loving* that, if it ever stopped, God would cease to exist, because *being*, for God, *is loving*. This is not a pious and schmaltzy *attitude*,

1. See Zizioulas, *Being as Communion.*

or *tenderness*, or *affectivity*, or personality *trait*, nor even simply an intentional act of the will; it is an *objective ontological fact*: it is not just what God does because he is *being nice*, or *morally good*, but rather: that's what God *is*, *the substance* or *hypostasis of loving*—the being whose *being is communion*. In other words, God's name is not a *noun* but a *verb*—a *hypostasized verb* or a *verb-become-noun*. The first layer or circle is always *circling*: it *is* the *Perichoresis* that God is. Should the *perichoresis* ever stop, there would be no God! That's all God is.

Incidentally, this objective, hypostatic understanding of love, is what explains why "the First Commandment," or rather the *only*, the *fundamental* commandment, from which all other moral or ethical imperatives flow, is love, because it is simply the *mode of being in which we are created*, so that, removing love removes being, life, in the final analysis *the possibility of human existence*.

Now the reason why we find it difficult to understand this is because we have had centuries and centuries of imaging being as the passive property of *individual entities* who first *are*, in themselves complete and independently self-sufficient even without action, and then, once there are several of these individual entities around, they end up in various sorts of relationships to each other. In an axiom of St. Thomas Aquinas, *operari sequitur esse*. The point of this assertion is that the nature of the operation or action is determined by the nature of the agent, the being. But it implies that being is prior to action, which we tend to take as self-evident.

Given such a fundamentally individualistic understanding of ontology, it has been logical for human beings to imagine that the ultimate being, the source and foundation of all being, is the ultimate single individual. Ultimate simplicity and unity then must be the perfection of God, on which all other reality is modeled; multiplicity is derivative and imperfect. And yet, the same Aquinas also maintained that "there is no real distinction between the divine *relationships* and the divine *essence*. For the divine Persons *are* in reality "subsistent relations."

Now, as the German theologian Karl Rahner has observed, while we have obviously *had* the doctrine of God's Trinity on the books for all these centuries, for all practical intents and purposes Christian lore could have continued unchanged if suddenly that doctrine had been dropped. So Geoffrey Wainwright has been able to report on "the ecumenical *rediscovery* of the Trinity" during the twentieth century.[2]

Wainwright also shows that this rediscovery has had everything to do with the Ecumenical Movement, in other words, with the increasingly joint effort of the Churches to clarify and realize the true nature of the Church. Because the Churches have realized that there is both a unity and a diversity among them, they have increasingly recognized the fact that the dynamic of the Trinitarian Communion in God is the source and model of how a multitude of persons, cultures, and particular churches are meant to reflect both the *undivided unity* and the *irreducible plurality* that is proper to God. And so, this is the second layer or circle, the Communion of the Church of churches, reflecting the pattern of the first layer or circle, the Communion of Persons in the Trinity.

But the Church is obviously not the final product. It is placed "in the world" but is not exactly identical with the world—there is something about it that is explicitly "not of the world." Yet it is taken "from the world," from real people who belong to the world and bring the world with them into the Church as they are plunged into the baptismal waters, into the Communion of Father, Son, and Holy Spirit, and then continue in the world in their new, ecclesial, Trinitarian being.

To follow the insight of communion ecclesiology, what has happened is that the original creation of the world, and of humankind in particular, modeled in perfect harmony on the Communion of the triune God, has been fractured by the autonomous breaking away of human self-will from God, creating an atomized sort of individualism and separatism, a world of competition, adversarial relationships, or no relationships at all, exploitation of

2. Reference unavailable.

humans by humans, and the ravishing of the earth. And since all creation, and humankind in particular, was created on the divine pattern of *being as communion,* once communion was thus fractured, *being, existence, life* itself, received a fatal blow. It is for this reason that "death is the wages of sin." The only way back to *life* then was restoration to *communion.* Hence the Church.

You see how this shift of emphasis to communion and relationality *as an ontological datum* moves us from the simply moralistic exhortation to being good and loving one another to the existential ultimatum of "*love or die*": the insight that, unless we recognize our essentially communal and relational nature, with each other and with the rest of the world around us, and act accordingly, we are executors of our own extinction.

And so it is that the Church can be seen as the recovered pattern of life and being for humankind and for all of creation, insofar as it emerges as reflecting the pattern and life of the Holy Trinity. What the world is, implicitly and potentially, in the divine design, the Church is meant to be *explicitly, sacramentally.* The Church then should be seen as the sacrament of the divinization and final recapitulation of all of creation, in and through Christ, to the Communion of God.

As a corollary perhaps we can note that such a communion ecclesiology is sometimes accused by various secularist and liberationist voices as being precisely what we said at the beginning we did *not* intend to be, navel-gazing, ecclesiocentric. In Vatican-II language, it has been said that this is a *Lumen gentium* type of ecclesiology, but it is doubtful whether it encompasses the vision of *Gaudium et spes* as well. In fact, to be more pointed, it could be suggested that this recapitulationist view, that the Church is here to engulf the world and restore it to the Trinity, is the one that leads to that imperialist and triumphalist attitude that precludes any positive respect for the world and for other cultures and religions, as they are. It is not dialogic but one-way missionary: it cannot learn, it can only teach; cannot listen, only speak.

This line of thinking is of course nothing new: it is in the well-trodden tradition of Antioch, which, in balance with the equally well-trodden tradition of Alexandria, is a wholesome warning against any kind of churchy complacency. I am taking Antioch as the paradigm for all theologies that insist on the distinction and virtual autonomy of the created from the uncreated, which, when exaggerated, produced Nestorianism, and Alexandria as the paradigm for theologies that see the fulfillment of all creation in being divinized and recapitulated to God, which, when exaggerated, produced Monophysitism.

While frankly admitting my personal preference for the Alexandrian leaning, I would like to suggest that a properly balanced communion ecclesiology is in fact the only radical and consistent theological foundation for a caring, nurturing, inclusive, and relational approach to the world, which can meet and empower all the legitimate economic, social, political, cultural, and environmental movements of our world today. It is a task for the upcoming generation of theologians to spell out all the practical implications of this, and to construct a particular and detailed theology for all these concerns that is rooted in the perspective of Trinitarian Communion, in understanding human life, social responsibility, and responsibility for the planet in terms of the relationality that grounds the existence and functioning of all systems.

Here we can only suggest *some key features* of such a theology. The Trinitarian paradigm is embarrassingly simple and obvious, almost simplistic. It basically suggests the structure of all reality as being a web of relations, in which there is both an inseparable, organic unity, connectedness, interdependence, on the one hand, and an irreducible diversity and plurality, which cannot be blended down into a homogeneous mass like a milkshake, on the other hand.

Applications. In any human community, nation, society, and then—explicitly—church, there is an organic unity, meaning that the life of the members depends on the web of relationships, the communion. So, rights and duties cannot—must not—be envisaged as individual, as it were out of the context of this web of organic relationships and interdependence. But, at the same time, personal uniqueness and diversity, or group diversity, must be affirmed rather than blended into homogeneity. The Church may preach these applications and collaborate in the social fabric to enhance them, but if it does not exemplify them in its own internal structures and behavior, putting into relief the Trinitarian Communion in diversity, then it fails in its iconic/sacramental function vis-a-vis the world.

One particular aspect of diversity-in-communion about which there are plenty of battles going on today is the matter of equality versus hierarchy. And it is obvious that the Trinitarian perspective can be used—or abused—in the service of opposite interests, and here a carefully and correctly crafted ecclesiology is essential, both for the Church and for its function vis-a-vis the world.

Part of the irreducible diversity is that you cannot level it off into a monochrome uniformity or "equality," in such a way that the unique functions or positions in the web of relationships disappears. Hence, perhaps less objectionable but synonymous with the word hierarchy is *order, orderedness* in this web of relationships. It is a very delicate job to work out the balance between equality, on the one hand, and order, un-confusable distinction of specific positions in the web of relations, on the other hand. The Three Persons of the Trinity are *equal* in their divinity, but the Father is not Son, nor the Son Father, and the Holy Spirit depends on both.

It took some centuries in the early history of Christianity to fine-hone a Trinitarian theology that was neither subordinationist, on the one hand, nor virtually unitarian, almost blending Three indistinguishable Persons into a monochrome unity of nature, on the other hand. In fact, two corresponding tendencies have survived, respectively in East and West, the former emphasizing the distinction of Persons and the initiatory role of the Father, the latter stressing their unity in the same divine nature. These two tendencies go hand in hand with corresponding ecclesiologies, and perhaps even political cultures. The Eastern emphasis on distinction and diversity in the Trinity is reflected in an ecclesiology of self-governing particular churches, which are in sacramental and faith communion, but are culturally quite diverse and jurisdictionally autonomous. The Latin West, on the other hand, has reflected its emphasis on unity of nature in the Trinity in a high degree of ecclesial uniformity and single jurisdiction, with a somewhat greater resistance to inculturation, to accepting diversity and self-governance.

As I have suggested, the patristic Church took a very long time to balance and fine-hone its Trinitarian theology; and it may be an even more challenging task for us to work out a number of orthodox models for reflecting that delicate balance between the meanings of equality and sharing in a common human condition, on the one hand, and recognizing, on the other hand, within this equality the myriad varieties and diversities of cultures, organizations, orders, and roles, none reducible to a uniform sameness, all accorded equal importance and dignity. If indeed the Church is a sacramental explicitation of the divine design for the world and for all creation, then this challenging task is not simply an internal matter of muddling through as best we can. Indeed, it is a priestly/ sacramental job we have "for the sake of the world."

To sum up, we can say that the communion character of the universe is an *ontological datum*, which by now has been demonstrated by the natural sciences as much as it is drawn from Trinitarian theology. The Church, in particular, is charged with putting this design into the clearest possible relief, and modeling the relationships that enhance being and life. It should be obvious that the foundation and key for all ethical principles governing both church and world in this enterprise is the interrelatedness of all, in their diversity, the respect, care, indeed the love that is the First Commandment, flowing very simply from the way reality is put together.

To put it bluntly, we must love—correctly—or die.

Bibliography

Althaus, Paul. *The Theology of Martin Luther.* Philadelphia: Fortress, 1966.

Afanasiev, Nicolas. *L'Eglise du Saint-Esprit.* Paris: Cerf, 1975.

Benedict, Saint. *The Rule of St. Benedict.* New York: Image, 1975.

Botte, Bernard. *La Tradition Apostolique de Saint Hippolyte: Essai de reconstitution.* Liturgiewissenschaftliche Quellen und Forschungen, Heft 39. Muenster: Aschendorff, 1960.

Dulles, Avery. *Models of the Church.* New York: Image, 1978.

Joint International Commission for Theological Dialogue between the Roman Catholic Church and the Orthodox Church. *The Mystery of the Church and of the Eucharist in the Light of the Mystery of the Holy Trinity.* In Paul McPartlan, *One in 2000? Towards Catholic-Orthodox Unity: Agreed Statements and Parish Papers,* 37–52. Middlegreen, Slough: St Paul's, 1993.

Kasper Walter. *A Celebration of Priestly Ministry: Challenge, Renewal, and Joy in the Catholic Priesthood.* New York: Crossroad, 2007.

Luther, Martin. *Luther's Works, vol. 35, Word and Sacrament.* Philadelphia: Muhlenberg, 1960.

McPartlan, Paul. *One in 2000? Towards Catholic-Orthodox Unity: Agreed Statements and Parish Papers.* Middlegreen, Slough: St Paul's, 1993.

———. *The Eucharist Makes the Church.* Edinburgh: T & T Clark, 1993.

Zizioulas, John. *Being as Communion.* Crestwood, NY: St. Vladimir's Seminary Press, 1985.

Ernest Skublics earned his Bachelor's Degree in Theology at the Benedictine School of Sant' Anselmo in Rome, his Master's Degree and Licentiate in Theology at the University of Ottawa, his Diploma in Liturgical Studies from the Trier Liturgical Institute in Germany, and his Doctorate in Theology at the University of Nijmegen in Holland, under the direction of Fr. Schillebeeckx.

He has been on the faculties of the University of Ottawa, the University of St. Michael's College in Toronto, and the Toronto School of Theology, lectured in various other universities and seminaries, was Associate Director of the Institute for Theological Studies of Seattle University, and finally Academic Dean of Mount Angel Seminary in Oregon, where he led the faculty in redesigning the theological curriculum based on the model of communion ecclesiology, inspired both by the Second Vatican Council and by the increasingly shared ecumenical understanding of the church. He was also founding President of the Canadian Liturgical Society.

He has written on subjects in liturgy, spirituality, ecclesiology, and theological education, in Canadian, American, Dutch, German, and British journals.